GOLDEN

 Empowering Rituals to
Conjure Your Inner Priestess

ASA SOLTAN

NORTH STAR WAY

New York   London   Toronto   Sydney   New Delhi

NORTH
STAR
WAY

North Star Way
An Imprint of Simon & Schuster, Inc.
1230 Avenue of the Americas
New York, NY 10020

First North Star Way hardcover edition May 2017

NORTH STAR WAY and colophon are trademarks of Simon & Schuster, Inc.

For information about special discounts for bulk purchases, please
contact Simon & Schuster Special Sales at 1-866-506-1949 or
business@simonandschuster.com.

The North Star Way Speakers Bureau can bring authors to your live event. For
more information or to book an event, contact the North Star Way Speakers
Bureau at 1-212-698-8888 or visit our website at www.thenorthstarway.com.

Interior design by Jaime Putorti

Manufactured in the United States of America

10 9 8 7 6 5 4 3 2 1

Library of Congress Cataloging-in-Publication Data is available.

ISBN 978-1-5011-5791-2
ISBN 978-1-5011-5869-8 (ebook)

This book is dedicated to my golden circle of Love. My Beloved Jermaine Jackson II, who is my king and my best friend, and our precious son, Soltan "Soul" Jackson, who was in my belly for the entire duration of writing this book. I cannot wait to hold you; you have been the most beautiful journey of my life. And to my incredible family, Mami Joon, Baba Joon, and Arta, who show me what unconditional love is every day and with whom I ride or die for for life. Also, to YOU, my gorgeous lovers. I am grateful for your continued support and energy. You lovers inspire me to keep going.

 CONTENTS

INTRODUCTION

was eight years old when my family fled our war-torn country of Iran. Overnight, the revolution that started the war transformed my country from the idyllic place of my childhood to a ravaged Islamic state with closed borders and regular bombings. The bombings always happened at night when it was pitch-dark outside. I spent those dark nights huddled with my family in the basement of our home, listening to the bombs falling with no idea where they would land.

When the borders finally opened again in 1984, my parents didn't waste any time. We left the next morning with a story about visiting my uncles in Germany for a week. Because we were expected to return to Iran only a week later, our luggage couldn't hint at the fact that we were really leaving for longer. We had one suitcase each to fill with our belongings, and we had to strategically choose what to pack.

We asked ourselves, *Should we bring things that will be useful or ones that are meaningful? Should we bring family pictures with us or should we take more clothes?* My parents couldn't bring their savings or jewels. They had to leave behind a huge number of the possessions they'd accumulated over the years, knowing they'd probably never be able to go back and get them. These included both valuable items and priceless family heirlooms.

None of us has stepped foot in Iran ever since.

Before we escaped, I remember how scared my parents were every time we heard the bomb siren go off. Seeing my parents live with that type of fear forced me to grow up a lot faster than most kids. But I think the most afraid I ever saw my parents was on the morning we left Iran. The airport was full of military, and we feared that someone would recognize my dad, who was a high-ranking naval official.

Luckily, as we approached the baggage checkpoint there was a huge commotion. The woman right in front of us was trying to smuggle her gold out of the country. Many people who were escaping from Iran wanted to bring their wealth with them, but this was not allowed. It was very different for us than it was for the families who left Iran before the start of the revolution in 1979. Those people—including many of the wealthy Persian families I later met in Beverly Hills—had been able to bring their money with them. Now it was illegal to bring valuables across the border.

The woman with the gold was immediately arrested, and though we felt for her, it was a lucky distraction. Busy dealing with her, the guards just waved my family through. This is one of the many reasons I love wearing so much gold—it's not only beautiful and sexy and gorgeous, but it also saved our lives. I still believe that gold protects me. Gold is magical, lover. Wouldn't you agree?

My parents breathed a small sigh of relief as our plane took off, but we knew we wouldn't truly be safe until we flew over the Iranian border. Until then, there was still a chance that our plane would be called back. When the pilot announced that we'd passed the border, everyone on the plane erupted into cheers.

All of a sudden, most of the women and girls on the plane simultaneously took off the veils they'd been forced to wear in public since the start of the revolution. I never really minded wearing the veil, so I didn't bother to take mine off, but it was striking to see dozens of women cheering as they joyously threw off their veils. This was the first time I realized what a big issue the veil was (and still is) for many women. My mother removed hers to cool off. As she hugged me close to her, I kissed her on her bare cheek. Then the stewardess walked down the aisle and handed me a coloring book and some crayons—a rare treat—and I felt like a child again for the first time in years.

It is during our darkest moments that we must focus to see the light.

—ARISTOTLE ONASSIS

To say that I experienced culture shock when we arrived in Germany would be a ridiculous understatement. Not only did I speak zero German or English, but I'd never really been around white people before. My family lived in England for a short time when I was really little, but back then I was too young to notice the differences between us. Until we arrived in Germany, I had no idea that people looked and acted and talked so different in other parts of the world. I'd naively assumed that everyone was just like us.

Va veila, was I wrong. My dad walked me from the tiny storeroom we were living in to school on my first day in Germany, repeating "*Ich heisse Asa*" to me over and over again. *My name is Asa.* By the time we arrived, those words were seared into my brain, but I was still completely unprepared for the reality check I was about to get.

My school in Iran had been like boarding school on steroids—superstrict and academic. Every morning, school started at seven, but we had to line up at six so the teachers could inspect our fingernails before class began. If our nails had dirt underneath or were too long, we'd get punished. We'd have to go to the back of the line, which was hugely embarrassing, and we had to go to after-school detention.

Walking into that German school was a huge shock. Not only were the other kids sitting around leisurely knitting instead of having their fingernails inspected, but they also all looked like aliens to me. In Iran, every girl looked like me, with a big nose, bushy eyebrows, huge hair, and a fuzzy semimustache. These kids were all blond and fair, but the thing that stuck out to me the most was how tiny their noses were. I had never seen a nose like that before, and suddenly they surrounded me.

As I took my seat in the back of the room, I realized that they weren't the aliens—I was. I was the one who was different. My hand instinctively went to my face, covering my nose and as much of my profile as possible, and I kept it there for the rest of the morning.

If you've seen even one episode of my TV show *Shahs of Sunset*, you already know that I've gone from hiding my nose in that German classroom to celebrating my ethnic features and voluptuous body. In fact, I'm so invested in the "Persian nose business," as I call it, that I got into major hot water with GG in Season 2 when I toasted to her boyfriend Omid's "big nose." So how did I find peace with myself and manage to hold on to it in the midst of so much drama and negativity?

The truth is that it has been quite a journey to evolve from that scared little girl in Germany to the confident, empowered artist, lover, and Persian Pop Priestess I am today. In Germany, I felt cast off from my land, my culture, and my people. My family was a lonely island in our tiny storeroom, and I longed for anything familiar, whether it was a glimpse of my grand-mother's face, the taste of authentic *tahdig* (Persian rice), or the sound of the daily call to prayer that emanated from the mosques across the city of Tehran.

Feeling a deep need to connect to my culture and myself, I began creating rituals that I practiced every day. At the time, these rituals were simply my way of taking a moment to create a sacred space and form an insular circle around myself so I could go within and remember who I really was.

What lies behind you and what lies in front of you, pales in comparison to what lies inside of you.
—RALPH WALDO EMERSON

As I grew and evolved, eventually becoming a refugee for the second time when another political upheaval forced my family to leave Germany and relocate to Los Angeles, these rituals kept me deeply connected to my golden Inner Priestess—the purposeful, authentic version of me that exists without ego, baggage, or attachments to material things. The truth is, we *all* have an Inner Priestess—even the guys who are reading this! It's simply the best version of who you are.

Today, I credit these rituals for my confidence, my unique style, my relationships, my career, my fearlessness, and my ability to not only survive war in the Middle East, but also to stay true to myself on reality TV! (Who's to say which is harder?)

Inner Priestess—the purposeful, authentic version of you that exists without ego, baggage, or attachments to material things. This is who you really are at your core, your divine inner self.

But you don't need to be a refugee, a TV star, or even a Persian to benefit enormously from these sacred, mindful rituals. These rituals can help you connect to yourself no matter where you are in life or where you're from. We all come into this world as pure golden lights with limitless potential, but after years of being told by our parents, our friends, society, and the media what we "should" look like, what we "should" do with our lives, and how we "should" act, layers of ego, insecurities, and confusion build up, dim our light, and hold us back from connecting with the perfect Inner Priestess who lives inside all of us.

The rituals in this book will help you finally break free from this baggage as you tap into your true purpose and power and start living the beautiful golden life you were meant to live.

The idea of practicing rituals may seem intimidating or foreign to you, but a ritual is simply any act that transforms ordinary life into conscious living. Many of us practice rituals all the time without even realizing that's what they are. Have you ever wondered why we blow out candles on our birthday cakes, walk down an aisle at our weddings, or wear black to funerals? These are all rituals that bring meaning to our lives and help us make sense of the overwhelming world around us. They mark new beginnings and give us an opportunity to heal from the past while acting with intention about the future.

We must let go of the life we have planned, so as to accept the one that is waiting for us.

—JOSEPH CAMPBELL

The simple rituals in this book aren't so different. By bringing you into a powerful state of pure presence, they can serve as catalysts for great change. Practicing them will bring divine energy into your daily life and empower your subconscious mind to manifest a whole new reality. In other words, you can use these rituals to create the life of your dreams. It's time to let go of the negative thoughts and relationship patterns that are holding you back and to uncover your unique and precious Inner Priestess.

Rituals used to be a part of everyday life, but they've mostly fallen by the wayside as technology and convenience have taken over. This makes it even more important to carve out time for some stillness and solitude. Our lives are so busy and our brains are bombarded by stimulation 24/7. We live on our phones and almost never consciously quiet our minds so they can rest. The result is that we don't learn to manage our thoughts, and they race uncontrollably with worries and anxiety like a monkey rattling his cage.

The other problem with our current lifestyle is that it includes almost no quality time with ourselves. We spend our days rushing around to get things done and "connecting" with our friends and family over social media, but we don't take the time to form a real connection with ourselves. How else can you get to know your true self and form a positive and loving relationship with the most important person in your life—you?

It takes work to turn yourself into a masterpiece, but lover, just imagine how stunning the final product will be. After a while, it won't feel like work anymore—it will just be fun, like spending time with your best friend. That's because the more work you do, the better you'll get to know yourself, and the more adept you'll become at managing your thoughts and your mind. The monkey will stop rattling the cage and you'll feel a golden inner glow radiating from your soul. *That* is the beauty of true confidence.

I'm so excited to finally share with you the rituals I've developed throughout my life. They will give you the tools to shed your toxic negativity and fear so you can connect to your Inner

Priestess and create the life you desire. Too many girls out there don't believe this is possible and can't even imagine living with this type of purpose and intention. I want to show you that with the right tools, it is possible for anyone.

When you have no purpose, it feels like your life doesn't count. You become insecure and hopeless, and your ego takes over, dragging you from one drama and bad relationship choice to the next. Does this sound familiar to you? Have you lost touch with who you really are and allowed society, the media, your parents, and the bullies at school to define you? The result may be a false image of yourself as being too much of this, not enough of that, and ultimately as being just not good enough.

No, *vaysa*! You are a unique being who is already in possession of everything you need to feel great about yourself and create your dream life. All you need to do is connect with your Inner Priestess and start manifesting your deepest desires.

So how can you do that? The first step is to clean the slate by wiping away the false beliefs you've built up over your true self throughout the years. Do you believe that you're too fat, too thin, too shy, too stupid, too poor, or too lazy to live the life you most want? Babe, trust me—none of that is true, and it's only after you shed that nonsense that you can finally get to the heart of who you really are.

To empty your vessel so you can begin filling it up with positive energy, love, and healing, we will begin with a lifestyle detox program. For one month you'll clean out your body, your environment, and your emotional life through daily visualization practices and rituals that will help you discover the genesis of your biggest issues and kiss them good-bye once and for all. It's when your mind and soul are cleansed that you can begin manifesting your deepest desires, and the following rituals will allow you to do this in every part of your life.

In order to evolve, grow, and improve your life, you have to be able and willing to be self-critical. That doesn't mean beating yourself up for your imperfections. Not at all, lover! But you must honestly examine various aspects of your life in order to shed light on the dark corners that need to be aired out and healed. Don't judge yourself for these dark corners. We all have them. Each of us is at a different point on our journey toward self-discovery. Be honest with yourself about where you are.

No matter how imperfect you may be, the more honest you are with yourself, the closer you'll get to your golden Inner Priestess. Honesty and loving self-criticism will help you reach the best you, manifest your destiny, and begin living the life you were meant to live. You'll finally accept your body and feel fully confident in your skin, manifest your soul mate, connect more deeply to your friends and family, and ultimately find your true purpose in life.

I consider myself lucky to have grown up in extreme circumstances that propelled me into a heightened state of awareness about myself, but I am far from perfect. I still struggle daily with fears and insecurities, and being on TV has forced me to face my demons in public on a completely different level. Throughout this book you'll read stories from my childhood as a refugee in Germany, my adolescence as a second-time refugee in Los Angeles, and even from behind the scenes of *Shahs of Sunset*. I hope that by learning more about my story you'll come to understand the impact these rituals can have.

Get ready and get excited. The power is yours to feel good again—maybe better than you ever have before—and the secret to having everything you want is finally within your reach. Whether you choose to address each area of your life simultaneously or one at a time, this book will give you the means to reach the Persian Pop Priestess's trademark state of glamorous, gorgeous mindfulness and begin living the life of your dreams.

My mission in life is not merely to survive, but to thrive; and to do so with some passion, some compassion, some humor, and some style.

–MAYA ANGELOU

When I was in college at UCLA, I worked part-time at an African art store in Santa Monica. One day, Maya Angelou came into the store. I have always been a huge fan of hers, and I was completely starstruck. She walked straight toward me, took my hands in hers, looked me directly in the eyes, and said, "Stay golden, my child."

This was a revelation to me. Maya Angelou saw something in me, and that filled me with the confidence and determination to use my life to make a positive impact. I want you to know that I see the same golden light of possibility in you. No matter where you are right now in life or what you're reaching for, I hope that my rituals will help you stop settling for anything that isn't worthy of you, start reaching your golden potential, and begin living the life of your dreams.

There is a voice that doesn't use words. Listen.

−RUMI

chapter one

PRIESTESS DETOX

Your pain is the breaking of the shell that
encloses your understanding.

—KAHLIL GIBRAN

PRIESTESS PREVIEW

In this chapter you'll learn all the steps of the Priestess Detox and how I came up with them, including:

EMOTIONAL DETOX

✦ Gratitude Ritual to shed negativity and get into the positive place where you'll thrive

✦ Self-Mythology Ritual to rewrite your story and gain control over your life

SOCIAL DETOX

✦ Energy Protection Ritual to shield yourself from negative energy

✦ Loving confrontation with negative people in your life to help raise their energy

PHYSICAL DETOX

✦ Connect to your food to cleanse your body and feel connected to nature

✦ Exercise to boost your confidence and energy

All together, these rituals are going to release your golden Inner Priestess and help her start to shine!

When I first started shooting *Shahs of Sunset* over six years ago, I was already on a spiritual path. For many years, I had been coping with life as a refugee by using my rituals to go deep inside of myself and reconnect with my core. This got me through all the challenges that had been thrown at me throughout my life, from being torn from my homeland as a child to being forced to leave my second home and face a foreign and unknown world yet again at the age of fifteen.

During those years, I went through a trial-and-error process to discover what helped me feel empowered. The details of the rituals I practiced may have shifted throughout the years, but no matter what I was going through, the process of taking a moment to stop, go within, and connect to my Inner Priestess always did the trick.

But this time, it wasn't working. Suddenly, I was thrust into a world that was brand new to me—reality television. Everything I said, did, wore, and ate was picked apart and criticized not only by my so-called friends on the show, but also by viewers around the world. This was strange and new for me.

Deep down, I knew I had the strength to get through this. At that point, I was pretty good at living outside of my comfort zone and staying true to myself in any environment. But this was *way* outside of my comfort zone—like, light-years away.

I was strong in my convictions, but my character was being tested. Big-time.

From the moment I began working on the show, it was important to me to be the same person on and off TV. It never even occurred to me to act any differently when the cameras were rolling. But once they did, I could see how my words and actions were often misconstrued and judged—and how much easier it would have been to put on an act.

This all started to weigh on me, and I began to feel physically and emotionally drained. My body was tired, and my spirit was hurting. I was thrilled to be on the show and inspired to dream bigger than ever about my future. But every time I shared my excitement with the people around me, they seemed determined to bring me down. I found myself surrounded by envy and competition. Some of the people who claimed to love me definitely were not happy about all of the good things in my life.

At the same time, I started to feel uncomfortable in my own skin for the first time in years. No matter how hard I tried, I couldn't seem to find time to make it to the gym, and as my physical fitness suffered, so did my emotional well-being. On the surface everything seemed to be going so well for me, but I found myself falling into a deep funk.

There was no way, though, that I was going to become a victim of my circumstances. Deep down, I knew who I was. I just needed a reminder. I tried practicing the rituals I had been using for years to connect to myself, but this time they weren't doing the trick. No matter how hard I tried, I couldn't get in there, to the very core of myself. It was as if there was too much stuff piled on top of that strong yet soft and vulnerable Inner Priestess that I knew was still in there, waiting to be uncovered.

If you always put limits on everything you do, physical or anything else, it will spread into your work and into your life. There are no limits. There are only plateaus, and you must not stay there, you must go beyond them.

–BRUCE LEE

We are all born pure and beautiful, with a unique purpose in this world. But then life takes a toll on us. We weigh ourselves down with the expectations of our parents, society, and the bullies at school. If we fail to live up to those expectations in any way, we internalize those messages and use them to create a false mythology about ourselves. Over time, we adopt this mythology as our truth. Most of the time, these stories are negative. They're about what we don't have and all the ways we aren't good enough. This lack and negativity becomes our focus. Eventually, it defines us.

But none of that is who you really are. You are not the things you do not have. You are not your imperfections. You are the perfect, whole creature who entered this world to be exactly who you are. And that person is still inside of you. You just have to get her out by shedding the layers of baggage that you've built up around you since birth and stripping down to the core of who you are.

Growing up as a Muslim woman of color, it was a huge struggle for me to ever feel like I was good enough. No matter where I went, I was so different from everyone around me, and it was easy to see those differences as negative and feel less than everyone else. I had worked so hard to maintain a healthy sense of self, but once I was thrust into the spotlight on *Shahs of Sunset*, all of those old insecurities started rearing their heads—and they were ugly!

On the show, I constantly felt the pressure to "reel it in" and portray myself as milder and more mainstream than I really was. Nobody really understood my vibe. The producers of the show meant well, but they weren't sure where to place me, so they lumped me into this category of "spiritual weirdo artist." And, sure, all of these elements are true to some extent. I am spiritual. My own mother (lovingly) calls me a "vierdo," and I have always expressed myself through my art. But none of those things define me. They're not who I am, and together, they don't sum me up. Unlike most people on TV, I couldn't easily be placed in a box and put on a shelf with a clearly understood label. I was complicated. I was real. And I was determined to stay that way.

It wasn't easy. Every single thing about me was being picked apart. Some people questioned whether I was thin enough to be on TV. Well, I have news for you, lover. I have never been thin, and I probably never will be. That's just not how my body was made. When we did promo shoots for the show, the wardrobe people never wanted me to wear the clothes I brought in with me because they were too funky and wild. Well, yes, I am funky and wild, thank you very much!

Of course, this was nothing compared to growing up with the fear of bombs falling on my house, but it felt like its own daily battle. There were more and more moments when I caught myself wishing I were more like this or less like that. It was clear that I needed to peel away these feelings and find the buried inner strength that I knew could sustain me.

It may sound strange, but when I was in the thick of this, I started thinking about Rocky running up the steps of the Philadelphia Museum of Art. (What can I say? I love movies.) I realized it was no coincidence that the epic montage of Rocky's training protocol included both a physical and emotional transformation. The mind, body, and soul aren't just connected; they're one and the same. There is always a mental and spiritual component to physical training—and vice versa. I realized this was why the stress from my social life was draining me physically and my lack of physical fitness was bringing my emotions down. It's all one. You can't compartmentalize any area of your life. Any meaningful change requires a full transformation.

I realized that I had a choice. I could waste away inside the bubble of negativity that was forming around me, or I could break free and cleanse my life of everything that wasn't serving me. Either way, it was up to me. That idea was incredibly empowering.

I hated every minute of training, but I said, "Don't quit. Suffer now and live the rest of your life as a champion."

—MUHAMMAD ALI

Realizing that you need to make a change and deciding to do it are the first and most important steps to getting everything you want in life. If you're sitting in a soup of negativity right now, I want you to know that you do not need to be there. No one but you can pull you out of it, lover. Isn't that amazing? You don't have to rely on anyone else to get you out of whatever situation you're in right now and into an amazing new reality.

As soon as I realized this about my own life, I began to develop what I refer to as my "Priestess Detox." This was my way of stripping down to the core of myself to get strong enough for the battle I was facing. I may not have felt strong enough in that moment, but I knew that my Inner Priestess was. I just had to let her out.

As I was coming up with the detox, I thought about how all of the world's major religions ritualistically practice some sort of fast. Buddhists fast on full-moon days and other holidays because they believe it is purifying and helps free the mind. Catholics abstain from eating meat on certain days to practice self-control. In Eastern Orthodoxy, there are many fast periods that adherents believe opens them up to God's grace. Hindus fast on new-moon days to purify themselves and enhance their concentration during meditation. In Judaism, there is a fasting day that is used to atone for sins. Mormons fast on the first Sunday of every month in order to feel closer to God. And Muslims fast during Ramadan to commemorate the revelation of the Qur'an.

Whether you're devoutly religious, an atheist, or anywhere in between, you can't deny the fact that all of these religions practice some type of fast for a reason. Most of them have been doing it for hundreds or thousands of years. Today it's common to do a juice cleanse or some other type of fast simply to lose weight, but these spiritual fasts that have been around for centuries have nothing to do with looks. They are an incredibly powerful way of cleansing the body and the spirit from the inside out, and I knew I needed to include that element in the Priestess Detox.

With faith, in full conscience, fasting calls women and men to an extra degree of self-awareness.

–TARIQ RAMADAN

But I knew right away that a one-dimensional physical detox wouldn't be enough to uncover my Inner Priestess. It wasn't just my body that needed change; it was every part of me. And I needed a three-dimensional detox to fully cleanse myself. So I added a social component. I had some friends who had been in my life for a long time, but I couldn't deny the fact that our every interaction had become negative and uncomfortable. When I shared things about my life with them, they made fun of my growth. This brought me down, and I could feel their negativity stunting me.

I was so conflicted. These friendships were treasures to me, but I couldn't let them continue to weigh me down. I ultimately decided to stay away from these friends during the detox so I could focus on myself and on getting stronger. Then maybe I would be able to protect myself from their negativity later.

The most important part of the detox, though, was the spiritual aspect. This consisted of emptying myself of all my insecurities and false beliefs so that I could touch my golden center and then mindfully fill myself back up. It became a full detox of the mind, body, and spirit. To change one of these elements, you must change them all. And you need to feel good in all three areas in order to feel good in any of them. You are one fluid being, not a bunch of disjointed parts. When your mind, body, and spirit are in harmony you will feel the confidence and joy that are your birthright.

The results of the Priestess Detox were so powerful that I started doing it twice a year and whenever I felt my old baggage piling up on me again. If it weren't for this detox, I'm not sure whether I would have been able to make it through five seasons (and counting!) on national TV while remaining true to myself, my family, my heritage, and my deepest-held beliefs. Not only did the detox help me rediscover my confidence, but it also has allowed me to keep getting stronger. Each time I do it, I manage to push farther ahead in all areas of my life and reach new levels of success and happiness. It has changed my whole life, and I can't wait for you to experience this, too.

This is a thirty-day detox. You'll read details for how to put all of the elements into practice in the next chapter. For now, let's focus on understanding the different components of the detox and how they'll cleanse your mind, body, and spirit from the inside out.

Perfection is not attainable, but if we chase perfection we can catch excellence.

—VINCE LOMBARDI

❦ PART 1—EMOTIONAL DETOX ❦

The fact that you have come this far means you are ready for improvement, progress, and change. Readiness and willingness are all you need to make this happen. You have arrived at that amazing place of readiness, which puts you way ahead of the game. Congratulations, lover. That is a huge accomplishment in and of itself.

Step 1—Focus on Gratitude

The Priestess Detox is all about shedding your mind, your body, and your spirit of any and all negativity, and you can't do that until you identify the negative things in your life. This may sound obvious, but uncovering the negative thoughts, people, and influences in your life can actually be a difficult process.

When you live with negativity and fear holding you back, it feels normal to you. It defines the way you think, the way you act, and the way you envision yourself and your place in the world. Of course, even if you're stuck in a negative place, not every thought and action is going to be negative. That would be too extreme. But when negativity infiltrates your mind, it is actually very hard to separate the healthy, positive thoughts from the negative ones.

That's what this portion of the detox is all about—discovering what negative thoughts and beliefs you're holding on to so you can finally let them go. Awareness is the first step. This can be really scary. It's hard to pull up that carpet and take a look at all the garbage and debris that's accumulated under there over the years. Your negative thoughts and beliefs represent your biggest issues and baggage, and it can be very painful to come face-to-face with them. But the truth is that you won't be able to move on from them until you do. The fact that you've decided to do this means you are ready and you can handle it. I know this is true, and I'm proud of you for getting to this point.

Change your thoughts and you change your world.
−NORMAN VINCENT PEALE

Negativity is poison. It saps your potential for greatness and is the very hurdle that keeps you from living a fulfilling and purposeful life. But unlike other obstacles in life like a physical handicap or financial hardship, negativity is completely up to you. You have complete and total power over it and can simply make the decision to become more positive.

This is amazing because it means you already have the tools to completely change your own life just by ridding yourself of negativity. You don't have to wait for anyone or anything else to shift in order to make a big change. When you realize that you want to make a change, you're admitting to yourself that it's within your power. It's a huge revelation to accept that you are responsible for your own life.

We are always fighting a battle between the positive and negative chatter in our minds. The trick is to turn the volume down on the negative voice in your head while turning the volume up on the positive one. They'll both always be there. It's unrealistic to believe you'll get to the point where you'll never have a negative thought again.

I'm not perfect, either. I still have negative thoughts from time to time, especially when my work is criticized. When I did a piece of performance art about the role of veils in modern Muslim culture on *Shahs of Sunset* that involved marching down Hollywood Boulevard with my girl gang, wearing a full veil, there were plenty of people who said, "That isn't art." Yes, it stung. I heard those negative voices, but I chose not to feed them.

Imagine going to the symphony and focusing all of your attention on hearing the delicate chime in the background of the orchestra instead of the noisy horns section. It's a choice. The horns will still be there, but if you focus and work hard at feeding the sound of the chimes, you will be able to tune the horns out. The stronger you become, the louder the chimes will get, and eventually that's all you'll hear. The same thing goes for your positive and negative chatter. Every day, you choose what to listen to and what to feed. Choose wisely.

As we express our gratitude, we must never forget that the highest appreciation is not to utter words, but to live by them.

—JOHN F. KENNEDY

Gratitude Ritual

Negative people are unhappy because they're so focused on what they *don't* have, whether that's certain looks, wealth, charm, fame, a particular lifestyle, or a partner. We take what we have for granted and think about what else we want. To some extent, we're wired this way. And it's wonderful to aspire to bigger and better things. I'm all for being ambitious. But we'll never be happy if we focus on the things we do not have. No matter how many of them we manage to get, there will always be something else out there to reach for. It's so incredibly powerful to just flip the switch and focus on what you *do* have instead of on what you don't. This simple practice is all it takes to change your mind-set from negative to positive.

I don't know you or the problems you're facing, and I would never diminish or discount them. Trust me, babe—I know exactly how hard life can be. But I also know that if you're reading this book right now, you have a lot to be grateful for, even if it's just a warm, safe place to sit and read, the money to purchase this book, the friend who loaned it to you, or the great local library you borrowed it from! Maybe it's just the fact that you're alive, breathing in gorgeous clean air. When you compare what you have with all the suffering in this world, it's easy to see that we all have so much to be grateful for.

Schedule a time to sit quietly by yourself with a journal and a cup of tea. Take a moment to shake out your body, releasing the stress of your day. Then sit down and take a deep breath. When you feel yourself entering the zone, begin to write down everything in your life that you're grateful for. Which people are you thankful to have in your life? What freedoms? What necessities? What little luxuries?

This is a very simple practice, but it dramatically changes the energy you're putting out into the world. This is not about the fake, over-the-top, clichéd gratitude we see all over social media that is really a subtle humble-brag. You know exactly what I mean. This is about the powerful realization that you are blessed, not telling the world that you are #blessed.

So many of us wait until we lose things to be grateful for them, but it's so much more powerful to be grateful for what you have right now. This helps you start living in gratitude, and that is the place where success and happiness thrive.

MY GRATITUDE LIST

To give you an idea of what I'm talking about, I'm happy to share my most recent gratitude list with you. Don't just copy my list! This is about you, not me. And don't you dare compare your list to mine and think that I have so much more to be grateful for. Stop and listen for that chime. What you have is amazing. You have so much to be grateful for.

Today I am grateful for:
My health
My family and their unconditional love and loyalty
My family's health
My beloved and his unconditional love
To live in a place where I have the freedom to be myself

The resilience to keep going

My passion that guides me

The courage to pursue my dreams

The kindness of strangers

My mother's intense dedication and love

My father's quiet strength and calmness in all situations

My brother's jokes that crack us all up even in tough situations

My fears, which allow growth and progress

The Internet, for allowing me to connect to the world

The gorgeous weather in Los Angeles

The sun that always brightens up my day

The moon, for mystifying me

Rumi poetry, for taking my soul to its home

Great music, for giving my days a soundtrack and for making me happy

---

Step 2—Take Your Life into Your Own Hands

The wound is the place where the Light enters you.

–RUMI

This portion of the detox is all about taking responsibility for your own life. Blaming someone or something else for all of the things you don't have is not only negative (and remember, we're trying to get rid of negativity), but it also allows you to be a victim in your own life. No matter what you've been through, you are not a victim. You are a powerful warrior who is in charge of what happens from this moment on.

Of course it's easy (and often tempting) to blame external circumstances for whatever we don't like about our lives. We've all been through things that have knocked us down. We can't control those things. But we get to decide whether or not we get back up.

My life was broken apart so many times. My home was taken away from me—twice. When we finally escaped from Iran, my family lost everything. We went from having a lot of money and being very comfortable to having nothing. We literally traded all of our money and belongings for our freedom. And when we finally got comfortable again in Germany, we were uprooted all over again.

It would have been easy for me to say "I can't go on" and allow myself to become a victim of my circumstances. But I had seen the way my parents handled all the obstacles we faced. No matter what was thrown at them, they never gave up. They woke up each morning, put on a smile, and worked hard to give my brother and me a better life. How different would my life (and theirs) be right now if they had given up and become victims in their lives? Just watching them, I learned lessons that were invaluable. I knew from a young age that if they could persevere in spite of everything, so could I.

Start by doing what's necessary; then do what's possible; and suddenly you are doing the impossible.

−SAINT FRANCIS OF ASSISI

When you allow yourself to be a victim, you are not living in a place of gratitude. You feel that life owes you something, but by not taking control you're actively keeping yourself from progress, growth, success, and happiness. It may feel sometimes like life is happening *to* you, but that is not true. Nothing and no one is responsible for creating the life you want but you. No matter what is thrown at you, you must rise up to the occasion and meet it. That's when the magic happens, because the universe or God or whatever force you believe in will reward you for having the courage to go after what you want.

Yes, this is superscary. It's a lot easier to pin your failures on someone or something else. But guess what? Failing at something and then blaming it on someone else doesn't make you any less of a failure! In fact, being brave and going for it doesn't make you a failure at all—even if you don't succeed. I believe that taking responsibility for your failures is the definition of success. It's being a victim and letting life happen to you that makes you a failure.

You have one life. What are you going to do with it? Will you sit there and blame everyone else for what you don't have, or are you going to take your life by the horns and ride it? The only reason I'm here right now is because I refused to be victimized. You might keep trying and failing, but if you keep going and never give up, you'll eventually get there. You just have to keep riding those waves and letting them crash over you. It doesn't matter how many times you get knocked down. All that matters is the number of times you get back up.

Keep your face always toward the sunshine—and shadows
will fall behind you.

—WALT WHITMAN

When we allow ourselves to be victims, we tell ourselves
stories about why our lives have gone a certain way. These are
excuses, but over time they morph into a full-on mythology
about ourselves, and the more we tell these stories to ourselves
and to the people in our lives, the more we believe them.

It's usually a lot easier to recognize these myths when you
hear them from someone else than when you tell them to yourself. Have you ever had a friend complain that there are "no good
men out there," while you watch her go after the absolute worst
men out there? Or have you heard family members explain that
they can't go after their dreams "in this economy" and watch them
settle for a soul-crushing corporate job instead? What about "My
parents got a divorce and that's why I have bad taste in men," or
"My boyfriend cheated on me, so I'll never trust again."

I call this your "schtick," and all it does is hold you back
from what you most want in this world. Ain't no one got time
for that. If there were really no good men out there, then everyone would be single. If all businesses were doomed to fail in this
economy, then no one would be making money. None of these
excuses are true.

The amazing thing is that you have the power to rewrite
your story. I know, I know. Right now, you might be thinking,
But my *story is different.*

Sorry, lover. It's not.

I'll give you an example of my own schtick and how I turned it around. When my family moved to Los Angeles, I was fifteen. We had no money. We lived in a tiny apartment in the slums of Beverly Hills. And there I was on my first day at the famous Beverly Hills High School, a politicized, feminist, artistic double refugee with crazy style.

For the first time since my family left Iran, the kids around me looked like me. In case you haven't noticed, there are a lot of Persians in Beverly Hills. Yet, I could not have felt more different from the rest of them. There were plenty of wealthy families in Germany, but the families in Beverly Hills had a whole different level of wealth and privilege. These kids hadn't worked for anything in their lives and didn't recognize the value of what they had. When I heard people gossip about all the Persian girls at Beverly getting a nose job and a beamer for their sixteenth birthday, I thought they were joking. I soon learned they were not.

Meanwhile, I had so little, but I knew that I had something those other kids would never have—a true appreciation and understanding of what really mattered. My family lived in a two-bedroom apartment, and my parents sacrificed their own comfort and slept on a pullout couch in the living room so that my brother and I could each have our own bedroom. I remember coming home late at night and trying not to wake my mom, who was asleep in the living room. She worked long double shifts as a nurse and desperately needed her sleep.

Yet I had my own moments of weakness. During my senior year, all of my friends went on a big graduation trip, but I couldn't afford to go. No one understood. They'd grown up with such privilege that they couldn't even comprehend the fact that I couldn't afford to go on the trip. But we had so little money that it was a big deal to me when I had five dollars to go to the movies or to put a little bit of gas in the car.

I knew that what I had was special, but it couldn't be measured the same way money could, and it was tempting to view the world in terms of what I didn't have. I tried to avoid this. As the years passed, I did my best to focus on gratitude and turn my problems into something beautiful. This fueled my art and made me the woman I ultimately became. But as I grew into an artist and entrepreneur, I feared that I didn't have the necessary tools to be successful. Unlike all the people around me, I had never learned about money or business from my parents. At the same time, I put a huge amount of pressure on myself to be successful in order to make my parents' sacrifices worthwhile.

Over time, I found myself resenting my parents for being so kind and caring. Compared to the cutthroat people I met in the business world, they seemed soft and weak, and I wished I had learned from them how to be a ruthless go-getter. I believed that I wasn't equipped to deal with the dog-eat-dog business world I found myself in, and I blamed my parents for this.

This became my false mythology schtick: *I am too weak to be successful. I don't have the skills I need to be an entrepreneur. I never learned how to run my own business. I am not good with money.*

It wasn't hard to see how this schtick was holding me back. This story gave me an excuse not to go after my dreams and ultimately to fail.

Finally, I used the ritual below to rewrite my story and focus on all of the wonderful things that my parents did teach me instead of the things they didn't. By example, they taught me how to be a good person, how to truly care for others, and how much more valuable love, compassion, and freedom are than money. That, I told myself, would take me a lot farther than simply knowing how to hustle.

My new narrative was all about the fact that I could become an entrepreneur on my own terms and run a business based on my values. I could be successful while staying true to myself. This was the story of my Inner Priestess. And as soon as I took on this narrative as my truth, it literally became true. I found more success than I'd ever previously experienced while staying true to myself. Even better, I became so much more grateful for my parents and everything they'd taught me. Their lessons became the building blocks of my spirituality and my strength. I owe everything to them.

There are two ways of spreading light: to be the candle or the mirror that reflects it.
—EDITH WHARTON, "VESALIUS IN ZANTE"

Self-Mythology Ritual—Rewrite Your Story
This exercise will help you take your life back into your own hands so you can actively walk toward success and happiness.

Sit down in a comfortable, quiet place. Put away your phone and anything else that might distract you and focus on getting into the zone. It is important to focus and be completely honest with yourself here. This can be challenging. We're all very attached to our schtick. It has in many ways formed our identities, and yet it's often the very thing that is holding us back from getting what we want in life!

In your journal, write down all the things that you believe have stopped your growth or kept you from success. Then add a list of the people who hated on you and blocked you from getting what you wanted. These situations and people can be from far back in your past or right now in the present. It's important to include anything and everyone who you believe has kept you from what you want, whether it's love, success, wealth, or finding your purpose in life.

After writing it all down, go through each item one by one and let it go. Free yourself from these chains that are holding you down. Read your list over, knowing that no person or event on this sheet of paper has any power over you. They cannot stop you. You are far more powerful than anything written on that paper, and yet you are holding on to these excuses for dear life. It's time to let them go so you can fly.

Once you feel that you have let everything on your list go, it's time to write a new story for yourself. This is the fun part. It's up to you to create a positive, empowering new narrative about who you are and what your life is going to be about. You can do this immediately after letting go of your myths or at another time. Either way, make sure you are in the moment and fully ready to take this on.

There are a few ways to do this. You can flip your former schtick on its head and write the opposite for each statement, or just start from scratch with a brand-new story. It's so easy and powerful to go from "I was cheated on and will never trust again" to "I was cheated on, and yet I rose up and am able to trust again." See that?

This can be as long or as short as feels natural. Use any form or type of writing you want. It can be bullet points or scribbled words or fully thought out paragraphs. The important thing is that your story is one hundred percent positive and puts you back in the driver's seat of your life—right where you belong.

We know what we are, but know not what we may be.
–WILLIAM SHAKESPEARE, *HAMLET*

PART 2—SOCIAL DETOX

Have you ever heard the saying that you are the average of the five people closest to you? People who hang out together tend to have similar salaries, outlooks on life, and even weights! This means even if you do all this work to become more positive and grateful, the negative people in your life can bring you right back down to their level. But the opposite is also true. By surrounding yourself with positive people, you can lift yourself up and raise your energy. This is the whole point of the social detox.

Step 1—Identify Negative People

Who are the negative people in your life? Who lifts you up, and who brings you down? Think about the five people you spend the most time with. They may be a combination of your family members, coworkers, a partner, and friends. How does it feel to think of yourself as the average of these five people? Does it feel good, or does it somehow seem wrong? If it doesn't feel right to you, read on. It's time to examine why you may be spending time with people who do not reflect the real golden you.

A viewer came up to me recently and said, "I know my husband loves me, but he's just so negative." While she was starting a new business, her husband ridiculed it and told her she was going to fail. Your gut reaction when reading this may be to assume he's just a jerk. But he clearly loved her. I saw that he wanted to protect her from failure by lowering her expectations. He meant well, but this type of negative attitude is still very dangerous.

It takes a lot of courage to express your dreams and to go after what you want. When you gather the strength to do this, you need encouragement from your loved ones, not negativity. Most of us already know exactly how likely we are to fail. We don't need to be reminded of that! Instead, we need help to protect our dreams like the delicate treasures they are. Remember, being negative doesn't necessarily make someone a bad person. Even the people who love you and want the best for you don't always understand your journey. That's okay. You can love them and have compassion for them while protecting yourself from their negativity.

Take a moment to stop and check in with yourself. Who can you talk to about your dreams? Who in your life encourages you, and who tells you that you're being unrealistic? Who are the people in your life who have the most power to influence you? Why do you give them this power?

Negative people are the naysayers. They're the ones who manage to hear whatever you say—positive or negative—and turn it into a problem. They never get excited about anything in their life or yours. Their lives are stagnant because their own negative energy is standing in their way of moving out of their comfort zone. Instead of moving forward with their own lives, they focus on telling you what to do with yours.

These people are energy suckers. Being around them is draining. If you don't yet have a clear sense of who the negative people are in your life, pay attention to who leaves you feeling drained and who energizes you. If you still can't tell, try telling the people in your life something exciting and see how they react. When people are miserable, other people's happiness makes them even more miserable because it forces them to face the things that are wrong in their own lives. But instead of rising up to meet you, they try to bring you back down to their level. Meanwhile, the people who are positive and empowered have no reason to tear down anyone else's dreams. They're too busy going after their own.

Happiness cannot be traveled to, owned, earned, worn, or consumed. Happiness is the spiritual experience of living every minute with love, grace, and gratitude.

—DENIS WAITLEY

Step 2—Protect Yourself from Negative Energy

Once you know who the negative people are in your life, you can protect yourself from their energy so it doesn't infect you. If this person or these people are not immediate family members or someone you have to see on a regular basis, simply try seeing them less often. If this is not possible, you can still protect yourself and your dreams. You don't have to cut the people you love out of your life, but you do have to be careful.

Our dreams are precious and delicate. Sometimes all it takes is one negative comment from an energy sucker to kill a lifelong dream. If you have someone negative in your life, stop sharing information about your dreams and passions with them. Let's say your mom is negative and stamps your flame out every time you see her. You don't have to stop seeing her; just find other things to talk about. The woman whose husband ridiculed her dreams didn't need to get a divorce, but I told her to avoid discussing her business with him as much as possible.

It's also possible to deal with these people by taking them with a grain of salt. This requires a lot of strength, though. When your father or sister or best friend starts listing all of the reasons you might fail, simply smile, roll your eyes, and go into another room. Don't let their negativity touch you.

Energy Protection Ritual

On reality TV, there's no way to completely avoid being around negative people. But it's very important to me to stop the negativity from impacting my life. I eventually created a ritual that I began to practice anytime I went into a crowd of people and before spending time with a negative person. Try doing this every time you are going to be around the people in your life you've identified as negative. It will dramatically change your energy and protect you from their negativity.

Sit quietly by yourself and close your eyes, imagining a white light of protection around you. This light forms a bubble around your entire being, extending out in every direction just a few inches away from your body. Picture yourself sitting inside of this bubble. It is transparent, but nothing can permeate it. Negativity cannot enter the bubble.

As you open your eyes and go on about your day, imagine that the bubble of white light is still there, protecting you. No matter who you see, what you hear, or what situations you may encounter, none of that negative energy can penetrate you.

Step 3—Have a Loving Confrontation

After a while, you will know whether or not you want to keep the negative people in your life. Keep in mind that when you become more positive and happy, some of these people may try to hold you back and may even become more negative. Eventually, you may have to decide to cut them out of your life.

Well, I am hereby giving you permission to do this. Sometimes, we have to take care of ourselves by staying away from people who are bad for us. This makes a lot of us feel guilty, but it shouldn't. You don't have to keep negative people in your life.

There's no need to make a big deal out of this and dramatically tell people that you are cutting them out of your life for good. Simply focus on spending more time with the people who help lift you up and less with those who bring you down. Now that you know the difference, it may become intolerable to spend time around negative people, anyway. You owe it to yourself to surround yourself with love and positivity. The energy that surrounds you is exactly what you'll become.

If the negative people in your life are immediate family members or important enough to you to keep them around, try having a very loving discussion about this without blaming or criticizing them. Try saying something like, "I love and appreciate you, and I want our relationship to be as strong as possible. I am working really hard on becoming more positive, and it would be helpful if you can try to keep your negative thoughts to yourself."

There is no way to know how people will react to this. Hopefully, they'll be open to it. Maybe they never realized how negative they were being and this will be a life-changing moment for them. But it's more likely that they'll be resistant. You can't go under trying to help someone else. However they react, it has nothing to do with you or your path forward toward finding your beautiful and perfect Inner Priestess.

PART 3—PHYSICAL DETOX

Your body is the vessel through which everything—good and bad—enters your life. It is virtually impossible for good things to happen in your life if you don't feel comfortable in your body and your skin. Your mind, body, and spirit cannot be separated from one another. So you must cleanse them at the same time.

Whenever there is a lot going on in my life, the first thing that usually suffers is my fitness. But this is such a vicious cycle. Things are blowing up in my life, I skip the gym, and then I stop feeling mentally and physically fit enough to deal with the stress I'm facing. When I actually make time to work out, I feel more resilient. The same thing goes for my eating habits. When I take the time to cook my own clean, wholesome food, I feel calmer and better prepared to tackle my life with energy and passion.

Step 1—Connect to Your Food

The rituals in this book are all about helping you connect to yourself and your life. The food you nourish your body with is a big part of your life, yet we so often disconnect from it and buy processed, packaged products that barely resemble food at all. Just as you must cultivate a relationship with your Inner Priestess, you need to form a relationship with your food.

If you've seen *Shahs of Sunset*, you already know that I love to eat. This physical detox is not about dieting or starving; it's about being more involved in your food. For example, I love French fries. They are my favorite indulgence, and, yes, I indulge quite often. But I also know just how I like them—crispy and really well seasoned. I kept going to restaurants and ordering fries and being disappointed until I realized that I wasn't taking an active role. I went home and started experimenting until I figured out how to make them exactly the way I like them.

Now, whenever I'm craving French fries I make them at home for myself. They're healthier than the ones from a restaurant, and I feel a satisfying connection to the delicious food I'm putting into my body.

When I was growing up in Iran, we didn't have every type of produce available all through the year. We ate what was growing locally during that particular season. In the summer, it was peaches, cherries, watermelon, and strawberries. In the winter, it was persimmons and pomegranates. I remember as a child feeling so closely connected to nature, and knowing that I was a part of something bigger than myself brought me a feeling of peace and happiness.

Don't get me wrong—I love going to Whole Foods and buying fresh pomegranates at any time of year, but I miss feeling that close connection to nature. I try to replicate it by going to the farmers' market every week and buying food that is grown locally from the same farmers whom I now recognize and know by name. No matter how busy my life is, I take this time to walk to the farmers' market and pick out food that I will then cook for myself at home. This has helped me feel connected to nature, my community, and myself.

I know this is not possible for everyone, but no matter where you live or what food you have access to, you can choose wholesome foods and cook them yourself. Throughout this detox, choose foods that don't have a list of ingredients—the ones that are the ingredient themselves. And pay attention to how eating this way affects your moods. Any time you can, try growing foods yourself in your garden, buying food from a local farm, or visiting a local farmers' market. This will get you back in touch with nature and bring you closer to your true inner self, where all the answers lie.

Put your heart, mind, and soul into even your smallest acts. This is the secret of success.

—SWAMI SIVANANDA

Step 2—Exercise

Remember, this is about detoxing your mind, body, and spirit, and anytime you're working on any aspect of yourself, it's incredibly important to exercise. You are a warrior, and your vessel needs to be in the best shape possible to face the daily battle of life. A lot of people would rather make excuses about why they can't find time to exercise than actually do it. If this is you, it's time to stop being a victim and start taking your body into your own hands. You need to be disciplined to find success in any area of your life, and that includes your physical fitness.

Trust me—I understand all of your reasons not to work out. Like I said, when things get busy my fitness is always the first thing that falls off. But it's also the very worst thing to let slide. You need to be physically strong in order to be emotionally and spiritually strong, and nothing in your life will change if you don't find time to make change happen.

Sit down and analyze your life and what you want to achieve. If this is important to you, there is always a way to shift things around so you have time to exercise. That doesn't mean it's going to be easy. I know it's easier to make excuses, but listen, babe—would you rather be a victim or someone who's in control of her life? This is the choice you are facing every day.

You are going to get some exercise every day during the Priestess Detox (all the details are in the next chapter). And I can't wait for you to see how much more radiant and powerful you'll feel.

You can start this detox today or continue reading the whole book and come back when you're ready. Trust yourself to know when the time is right for you to begin. When it is, get excited for the next thirty days to revolutionize your entire life. Your Inner Priestess awaits!

Let your life lightly dance on the edges of Time like dew on the tip of a leaf.

—RABINDRANATH TAGORE

chapter two

PRIESTESS PLAN

Yesterday is but today's memory, and tomorrow is today's dream.

—KAHLIL GIBRAN

PRIESTESS PREVIEW

This chapter will give you all the details about which rituals to complete during each week of Priestess Detox:

WEEK 1

Daily Rituals

✦ Morning Meditation

✦ Evening Meditation

✦ Daily Cooking Ritual

✦ Morning Movement Ritual

✦ Gratitude Ritual

✦ Identify and Avoid Negative People

Every-Other-Day Ritual

✦ Exercise Ritual

WEEK 2

Daily Rituals

✦ Morning Meditation

✦ Evening Meditation

✦ Daily Cooking Ritual

✦ Morning Movement Ritual

✦ Identify and Avoid Negative People

Every-Other-Day Ritual

✦ Exercise Ritual

Onetime Ritual

✦ Self-Mythology Ritual

WEEK 3

Daily Rituals

✦ Morning Meditation

✦ Evening Meditation

✦ Daily Cooking Ritual

✦ Morning Movement Ritual

✦ Energy Protection Ritual

Every-Other-Day Ritual

✦ Exercise Ritual

WEEK 4

Daily Rituals

✦ Morning Meditation

✦ Evening Meditation

✦ Daily Cooking Ritual

✦ Morning Movement Ritual

✦ Energy Protection Ritual

Every-Other-Day Ritual

✦ Exercise Ritual

As-Often-as-Needed Ritual

✦ Loving Confrontation

This is going to be a life-changing month for you! At the end of it, you'll be brimming with confidence, energy, and power, ready to take on the world like the golden warrior that you are deep down inside.

You just read a lot of information about how I came up with the Priestess Detox and what it's done for me. Now it's time to put it into practice in your own life. There are some rituals and practices that you are going to do every day and others that you will only do once. This will not be that time-consuming, but it will require a lot of your mental energy. Try to do this during a month when you don't have any major projects due at work or school or anything going on that will require too much of your attention.

No excuses, though, lover! If your life is always crazy, then it's even more important that you do this, so pick a time that makes the most sense for you and stick to it. The rest of the rituals in this book will be more effective if you do them after the detox, when your Inner Priestess is freshly cleansed and ready to party. Let's get started!

Gratitude is the fairest blossom which springs from the soul.
–HENRY WARD BEECHER

 WEEK ONE

Daily Rituals
Do each of these every day this week.

Morning and Evening Meditations

These two short but meaningful meditations have the power to transform your life. Just taking a moment to check in with yourself at the beginning and end of the day is a surprisingly powerful way to connect with yourself and discover what is fueling you, what is draining you, and what you need to do to go farther.

Morning Meditation

A major focus this month is going to be creating a meditative space for yourself to get in touch with who you are at your core. To do that, it's important to touch base with yourself in the morning before you do anything else. Read that last sentence again, lover. I said, *before you do anything else.* That includes looking at your phone to see what's going on in the world or on social media.

So many of us grab our phones as soon as we open our eyes in the morning. I'm guilty of this, too! But this puts you in a reactionary mode right away. Before you take time to actively plan your day or set your intentions, you are reacting to the latest news, messages from work, and your friends' selfies. Starting the day this way can set off a chain reaction of . . . reaction! Just as what you eat for breakfast can set the tone for how you eat all day, what you do first thing in the morning can set the tone for how you'll act and react all day. Being in control of your life means taking intentional, well-thought-out action, not reacting wildly to whatever is happening on your phone.

Instead, sit up. Take a moment to stretch your body out, and then go to a place in your house that feels safe, quiet, and comfortable. I like to make myself a cup of tea and sit on the terrace. Sit down, close your eyes, and just check in with yourself.

How are you doing? What's going on with you right now? Take an honest accounting of the status of your life. How do you feel physically? Are you tired? Why do you think you're tired? Do you feel pain anywhere? Are you energized? Simply notice, don't judge.

Then move on to your emotional state. How do you feel about your life this morning? Is this the life you want right now? If not, what do you want? And what do you need to do to get it? What is the next step you need to take?

Once you have a vision for your future, you should try to see it in your mind as often as you can. Take a minute here to visualize that future. Picture yourself on the beach rocking that killer bikini. See yourself kicking ass in your dream job, or standing at the altar with your beloved. Enjoy seeing your greatest dreams playing out in your mind. The more you see the life you want, the faster you can move toward it.

This practice of doing a regular check-in is nothing new. Presidents address the country every year during a State of the Union address. Before a sports game, the coach gathers the team to check in. Most offices and companies hold a weekly status meeting. It is so important for members of every sort of team to check in with one another regularly and make sure they are on the same page.

We do this in every aspect of our lives, yet we never take the time to get on the same page with ourselves. We go through our days like robots, and everything we do is out of either obligation or habit. The morning meditation will help you start the day with purpose. This is how you'll take back the power to drive your whole life. How are you going to achieve anything without first thinking it through? This is your chance to do that. Take it.

I know how hard it is to find even five minutes some days. But when you carve out those five minutes no matter what else is going on, you're telling God or the universe that you honor yourself and are claiming this time for yourself. That is powerful, and if you have the strength to do this, you're eighty percent of the way there.

Evening Meditation

While the morning meditation is a general check-in, my evening meditation is specifically about one area of my life that I'm working on at the moment. The moments before you go to sleep and right after you wake up are the most powerful times of the day. While the morning is a good time to get empowered and energized, the evening is more mystical. This is when the magic happens.

Every night before bed, return to your comfortable seat and get into the zone. Pick one aspect of your life that you want to focus on. Maybe it's a project at work or a relationship you're struggling with. Maybe it's the Priestess Detox you're doing! No matter what it is, taking five minutes before bed to focus on it will help you move through it with ease.

Close your eyes and think about the challenge you're dealing with. What is happening? Maybe you're struggling to lose the baby weight or having trouble paying your bills or getting out of debt. Perhaps you feel stuck in your career. Why do you think this is happening? How do you feel about it? What do you think is making you feel that way? Take a moment to think about the next steps you need to take. Where do you want those steps to lead? Visualize your ideal resolution. How can you make that happen?

You can focus on the same thing every night during the detox or choose to think about something different each night. It's up to you. The important thing is to get specific with yourself so that you are closely in touch with what you want and how you can get it.

Meditation is the soul's perspective glass.

—OWEN FELTHAM

Daily Cooking Ritual

For the thirty days of the detox, you are going to avoid processed foods, sugar, and alcohol. Don't panic! There is still a ton of delicious food you can eat. If you're freaking out about abstaining from alcohol for a month, that means you probably really need to do it. As you may have seen on *Shahs of Sunset* (ahem), alcohol makes you more likely to react emotionally to every little thing. This month is about taking calm, intentional action, not reacting, and being under the influence of alcohol makes it almost impossible to do that. It's only a month. You'll live.

Every day this month, cook at least one meal for yourself. It doesn't matter if it's scrambled eggs for breakfast or a gourmet meal for dinner. Make the time and space to connect to your food and prepare it for yourself. If you're not accustomed to cooking for yourself, get excited about trying something new! Treat yourself to a new cookbook (or borrow one from the library) and enjoy poring over the recipes to find something that you like.

You probably already know how much I love to cook. It's the only thing I enjoy even more than eating! Besides French fries, my favorite foods to cook are the ones that I remember eating as a child. They help me feel connected to that sacred, innocent time of my life. Have you tried making some of your childhood favorites? This is a great way to connect to yourself while doing something good for your mind, body, and spirit.

Morning Movement Ritual

You can do this right before or after your morning meditation—whatever works best for you and your life. It's important to wake up your body in the morning and get connected so that you are ready to face whatever the day holds. When I was developing the Priestess Detox, I asked a lot of the most successful people I know about what they do first thing every morning. I was fascinated to hear that the vast majority of them get up early and go for a run no matter what else is going on in their lives.

I'm going to be honest with you, lover. This is not for me. My body was not made for running! I'd rather dance, swim, practice yoga, walk, stretch, or make love with my beloved. But that doesn't mean that I can't benefit from a morning movement ritual. Every morning, I do several sun salutations. If I'm busy, I do them in my bedroom right next to my bed before I start my day. If I have more time, I go outside and do them underneath my olive tree.

If you're not familiar with sun salutations, they're a sequence of yoga poses that energize your body and work every major muscle group. It's a beautiful way to start the day, and researchers believe that ancient civilizations started their days this way up to ten thousand years ago. Anything that's been around that long obviously has value, and I feel so much more energized when I start my day this way.

If yoga isn't your thing, that's fine, lover. Find a different morning ritual that works for you. The best options are yoga, walking, or running for twenty minutes every morning. No excuses! Find a way to work this into your own life. Maybe you already take your dog for a walk every morning; if so, build onto that. Maybe you drive to Starbucks to get your coffee. Can you walk or jog there instead? Can you walk your kids to school instead of driving them? You don't have to do the same movement ritual every morning. Maybe one day you feel like doing yoga and the next morning you have more energy to go for a jog. Make this work for you.

On the weekends, instead of my morning yoga, I wake up early and treat myself to a long walk on the beach with my beloved. I always come back home feeling completely refreshed and recharged. Your morning movement ritual will do the same thing for you.

Gratitude Ritual

This week you're going to focus on gratitude to shift your energy from negative to positive. Do the gratitude ritual on page 28 every day this week. You can do it right before or after your morning or evening meditation or at a separate time. Your lists may be redundant, or maybe you'll find new things to be grateful for each day. Either way, taking the time every day to practice gratitude for the good things in your life will have a profound impact on your mood and your overall energy.

Identify and Avoid Negative People

This week start paying attention to who the negative people are in your life. Once you become aware that someone is negative, try to avoid him or her for the rest of the detox. I know this isn't always possible, but do it when you can. You'll learn how to deal with everyone else later.

Every-Other-Day Ritual

Exercise Ritual

In addition to your morning movement ritual, it's important to work out at least three times a week. I try to go to the gym three to five times a week no matter how busy I am. It is so important to keep my energy up and my mind focused and sharp.

You already know I don't diet. I eat really healthy, but I eat a lot, so I *have* to maintain a regular exercise routine. I'm going to share mine with you below. You can follow this one or find a different one, but it's important that you find a routine that works for your body. Everyone knows how good it feels to work out. It gets endorphins pumping and gives us a natural high. Plus, most of us spend a great deal of time in our heads, so we have to get physical on a regular basis to balance it out. The Priestess Detox is all about balancing your mind, body, and soul. You can't do that without regular exercise.

A ton of fans ask me about my exercise routine, so I'm excited to share it with you here. If you aren't exercising regularly already, you may want to check with your doctor before starting to make sure you are healthy and in good shape to begin exercising. And remember, you don't have to follow exactly what I do. Find a workout routine that works for you and your body. You're the one who matters! If you're not familiar with any of the exercises I mention here, there's a ton of good information online about specific workout routines for every body.

First, I stretch out my whole body, and then I do thirty minutes of cardio to get my sweat on and my heart pumping.

This can be jogging, biking, or doing the elliptical machine or StairMaster—whatever works for you.

Then, three times a week I work on my glutes and legs. This is a must for me. I'm naturally bottom heavy. Don't get me wrong— I like to be thick, but in order to feel good in my body I have to make sure my bottom half is toned. I'm lucky because I inherited my mom's booty. She and her sisters all have the same booty. It's huge and toned and sits up nice and high even though she doesn't exercise at all. But I want to make sure mine stays that way, so I spend lots of time working on my booty. The best thing for this is squats. If you have a big booty like me, this will help you tone it up. Even if you have a flat butt, this will give you a cute little bubble.

LEG WORKOUT

+ Squats: 3 sets of 20 reps with 20–30 pounds of weight

+ Lunges: 3 sets of 20 reps with 5- to 8-pound hand weights

+ Leg Presses: 3 sets of 20 reps with 30 pounds of weight

+ Inner and Outer Thigh Presses: 3 sets of 20 reps each with 30 pounds of weight

Two times a week, I work on my arms and back. I'm not gonna front, babe. I totally slack on these days. I just don't like doing these exercises as much, but these are my problem areas. I have a wide back and big arms, so I have to work on them. I use very light weights so that I don't bulk up, but you can use heavier weights if you're naturally more petite.

ARM/BACK WORKOUT

✦ Bicep Curls: 4 sets of 25 reps with 5- to 8-pound hand weights

✦ Shoulder Presses: 4 sets of 25 reps with 5- to 8-pound hand weights

✦ Arm Lifts: 4 sets of 25 reps with 5- to 8-pound hand weights

✦ Lat Pull-downs: 4 sets of 25 reps with 20 pounds of weight

✦ Tricep Kickbacks: 4 sets of 25 reps with 5- to 8-pound hand weights

✦ Tricep Extensions: 4 sets of 25 reps with 20 pounds of weight

Then, every time I go to the gym, I work on my abs. This is a must for me! I really see a big difference when I do this, which motivates me to keep going.

AB WORKOUT

I lie on a bench holding a 12-pound weight. With my legs lifted high, I lift my chest up toward the sky while holding the weight. I do two hundred of these. They are killer! Then, if I'm feeling really ambitious, I also do a hundred scissors. Sorry, lover, but you're not going to get rocking abs without putting some work into it. But I know you can do it.

Then I stretch out my whole body—this is super important. Always stretch before and after you exercise. This may seem like a lot, but it adds up to about an hour of exercise each time I go to the gym. You can start more slowly if you like, but you must get some exercise if you want your body in the shape you need to carry you powerfully through this life.

WEEK 2

Daily Rituals

Continue to do the following rituals each day:

Morning Meditation
Evening Meditation
Daily Cooking Ritual
Morning Movement Ritual
Identify and Avoid Negative People

Every-Other-Day Ritual

Exercise Ritual

Onetime Ritual

In addition, this week set aside time to do the self-mythology ritual on page 36. You can stop doing the gratitude ritual each day or keep going if you enjoy it! I like to do a miniversion each night by sharing with my beloved three things that I'm grateful for.

WEEK 3

Daily Rituals

Continue to do the following rituals each day:

Morning Meditation

Evening Meditation

Daily Cooking Ritual

Morning Movement Ritual

Energy Protection Ritual—Your new ritual this week is the energy protection ritual on page 41. By now, you probably have a good sense of who the negative people are in your life. You may be successfully avoiding some of them, but maybe you still have to face some of these people on a regular basis. This week, any-time you think you might end up in the same room as someone you've identified as negative, do the energy protection ritual first.

Every-Other-Day Ritual

Exercise Ritual

 WEEK 4

Daily Rituals

Continue to do the following rituals each day:

Morning Meditation

Evening Meditation

Daily Cooking Ritual

Morning Movement Ritual

Energy Protection Ritual

Every-Other-Day Ritual

Exercise Ritual

As-Often-as-Needed Ritual

Loving Confrontation—Your new challenge this week is to have a loving confrontation with a negative person whom you want to keep in your life. Using the suggested language on page 43 or your own words, compassionately and honestly tell this person how you feel. Remember, you are strong enough to handle his or her reaction, even if it's angry or negative. That has nothing to do with you. Whether or not this person changes his or her ways, you can continue to get stronger and become better able to protect yourself from his or her negative energy.

That's it! It sounds simple (and it is), but there may be some tough moments this month. Anytime you change your way of doing things, your deepest issues will rise to the surface as if they're fighting off the change. Of course, that's the whole point of the detox. You want those issues to rise up so you can look them in the face and beat them away. But sometimes it's painful to see all of the hurt, negativity, and resentment that you've been holding on to for all these years.

If this happens to you, use the daily rituals to move through the difficulties and remember that they will pass quickly, but only if you keep going. Whenever you're tempted to stuff your issues down and ignore them, remind yourself that this will only make them grow bigger. You are stronger than those issues. They are not who you are, and after you complete this detox they will no longer define you.

At the end of the month, you will probably feel a deep inner peace, happiness, and power. Use that new energy to propel yourself through the rest of the rituals in this book and watch the rest of your life transform.

Gratitude unlocks the fullness of life. It turns what we have into enough, and more. It turns denial into acceptance, chaos to order, confusion to clarity. It can turn a meal into a feast, a house into a home, a stranger into a friend.

–MELODY BEATTIE

chapter three

RADIATE BEAUTY FROM THE INSIDE OUT

That's how powerful you are, girl . . . You pretty, but pretty alone is
not what people see. You the kinda pretty, the kinda beauty, that's like
a mirror. Men and women see themselves in you, only now they so
beautiful that they can't bear to see you go.

—WALTER MOSLEY, *THE LAST DAYS OF PTOLEMY GREY*

PRIESTESS PREVIEW

In this chapter, you'll learn how to complete the following rituals:

✦ Beauty Bath Ritual

✦ Priestess Power Shower

✦ Vibe Out

✦ Snap a #SelfLoveSelfie

Completing these rituals will fill you with inner confidence that will shine through the golden light of your eyes.

For me, beauty was defined by my early childhood in Iran. Before the revolution and the start of the war, my life was peaceful, idyllic, and very beautiful. My parents both came from big, close-knit families, and I was constantly surrounded by dozens of aunties, uncles, and cousins my own age. It was always sticky and hot out, but the river just outside of Tehran somehow remained cool. During our weekly family picnics, my cousins and I tied bottles of Coca-Cola together and plunged them into the river along with a whole watermelon to be cooled. After we swam, danced on the riverbank, and ate our lunch, it was pure magic to bite down on a cold piece of watermelon and chase it with an icy slug of sweet, bubbly Coke.

When we weren't at school or out picnicking, my grandmother and aunties took my girl cousins and me to the local bathhouse, which we called the *hammam*. It was so beautiful there, with its domed ceilings, marble floors, and mind-blowingly intricate mosaics. No matter how many times I'd been there, the sheer size of the space, the warmth of the air, and the powerful scent of roses overwhelmed my senses. The hammam was like an ancient spa—all steamy and rosy and warm. From the outside, it looked like a mosque. Inside, it was all made of marble with radiant heating underneath. I'll never forget the sensation of walking with bare feet over the warm white marble.

Going to the hammam was something I always looked forward to. It was a social place. My cousins and I took turns scrubbing and shampooing each other while our aunties gossiped with their friends and caught up on each other's lives. None of us had any shame about our bodies. As far as we knew, we were perfect.

Looking at my cousins was like looking in the mirror. We all had the same thick limbs, black hair, and strong features, and our mothers wore their aging versions of those traits with grace and dignity. There was comfort in our sameness, and I eagerly looked forward to our visits to the hammam each week. No matter what sort of mood I was in beforehand, the mere scent of the rose oil soothed me, and immersing myself in the bath always made me feel reborn.

I didn't realize it at the time, but these were my first experiences with rituals, ones that I would return to in my mind again and again when all that sameness and comfort was taken from me.

Beauty is not in the face; beauty is a light in the heart.

–KAHLIL GIBRAN

My first day of school in Germany was the day my relationship with my self-image changed forever. Walking into the classroom, I quickly scanned the sea of fair-skinned faces in front of me, taking in how different they were from everything I was used to. Their hair, skin, noses, cheekbones, and even bodies were antithetical to mine, and for the first time I asked myself the question that every girl I know has asked herself at some point in her life: *Am I ugly?*

Just like that, the features I had never given a second thought to before weren't good enough anymore. My hair was too big, too black, and too kinky. My eyes were too dark. My features were too loud. And my body! *Va veila*, it was all wrong, too. The other girls had thin, delicate limbs. They looked like lovely, frail birds, while my legs and hips were already sturdy and thick. *Too* thick, I immediately decided, and over the next few weeks I did everything I could to hide all of the things that made me feel *zesht*, or ugly.

I sat in the back of the room with my hand curled against the side of my face to shield my profile from my classmates' eyes. I wore baggy clothes to conceal my frame, and every night I sat in front of the mirror in my family's tiny storeroom and experimented with different hairstyles, trying to find one that would make my hair look like the other girls'. Of course, it was hopeless.

At the time, bangs were really in style. I wanted to fit in, so I tried to cut bangs on myself, but because my hair is so thick and textured, my bangs curled up into a big frizz ball. They were hideous. I can laugh about it now, but at the time it was painful to be so different. I desperately tried to force myself to fit in with the trends instead of finding a style that fit with me.

PRIESTESS POWER POINT:
THE MIND FOLLOWS THE BODY

We all know that smiling can actually lift your mood and make you feel happier. It also boosts your confidence when you're feeling down about yourself. The same thing goes for your posture. When you're not feeling great, slouching can make you feel even more depressed. Who needs that? The next time you're feeling ugly or insecure, sit up with your neck straight, your chest up, and your shoulders down, and think of something silly or funny or sexy that makes you smile. Fake it if you have to! You'll instantly feel better and you'll start to radiate that inner joy and confidence.

Gymnastics class was the worst part of my day. We had to wear form-fitting tights and leotards, and for that hour I couldn't hide my well-developed body underneath layers of baggy clothes. It was on display right next to the lithe German girls. But, strangely, gymnastics was also where I thrived. My thick, athletic legs gave me an edge. I was stronger than the other girls. Little by little it dawned on me that I could use my differences to my advantage. Maybe the things I thought were my greatest weaknesses could actually be my greatest strengths.

It was at gymnastics class that I heard for the first time the German girls complain about their own bodies. They were insecure about how skinny they were! The irony of this was not lost on me. If they wanted what I had, why should I waste my time and energy wishing I had what they had?

This is a trap that women fall into far too often. We compare ourselves to those around us and come to believe that whatever we have is not enough. We're not thin enough or curvy enough. Our hair isn't thick enough or shiny enough. Our noses aren't small enough. We're not smart enough or cute enough, and at the end of the day we just. Aren't. Good. Enough. *Basseh!* Whatever you have, whatever you are—it is enough. It is more than enough, actually, but the first step to owning that is accepting the fact that in this moment you are simply enough.

As if you were on fire from within. / The moon lives in the lining of your skin.

—PABLO NERUDA, "ODE TO A NAKED BEAUTY"

I finally learned to embrace the fact that I was enough by thinking about my beautiful grandmother and aunties in Iran. When I was alone in the shower and no one could see or hear me, I closed my eyes and imagined that I was back at the hammam with my cousins. In my mind I could smell the rose oil and hear the women's laughter, and for a moment I was that innocent little girl again. Connecting to those happy memories reminded me of who I really was—not this ugly, insecure girl but the beautiful, happy girl at the hammam. If I was enough back then, maybe I still was.

I repeated this ritual every time I took a shower, telling myself over and over "I am enough," until I slowly started to believe it. I stopped hiding my body behind baggy clothes and no longer covered up my nose in class. For the first time since leaving Iran, I actually wanted people to see the real me.

Priestess Power Point: Feel "Scentual"

Wearing a scent that you like actually boosts your confidence. Experiment with different scents until you find one that feels right to you, and every time you catch a whiff of yourself, your confidence will rise. Next, find ways to incorporate this scent into little rituals that you can practice throughout the day.

Rose oil has always been my signature scent. Every time I smell it on myself, I feel sexy, powerful, and purely like me. To lift my mood when I'm feeling down, I put rose water in a spray bottle and keep it in the fridge. When I need it, I spray the rose water on my face and instantly feel refreshed and rejuvenated. Try this with your own signature scent for a confidence boost whenever you need it!

Now it makes me laugh to see that all the features I was so insecure about as a kid are fashionable. Other girls are going to extreme lengths, including getting surgery, to obtain them. Thanks to JLo and then Beyoncé and Kim Kardashian, girls today want my muscular thighs, big butt, thick eyebrows, and lush hair. Thank goodness I didn't try to change myself back then! If there's something you're insecure about, trust that it will probably be "in" someday, too. The very things you may hate about yourself will be the bomb at some point, so you might as well learn to embrace them now and let the trends catch up with you.

What's that one thing you can't stand about yourself? Is it your small boobs, your thick calves, or your small stature? For me, that thing was always my *bene*, my nose. But now my nose is my signature. It's who I am. I have bold ethnic features, and a small nose would look completely out of place on my face. If you embrace your perceived flaws instead of trying to hide or change them, they, too, can become your trademark. You can be the girl who rocks that sexy low neckline with no bra, the queen with the baddest kicks on the soccer team, or the small but mighty powerhouse who fills the room with her positive energy.

Nobody else has what you have. Focus on improving yourself within your element, using to your advantage all of the things that make you unique. When I stood there in my leotard on my first day of gymnastics, I could not have felt any more ugly or less feminine. I thought my wide hips made my body look the opposite of girly. But now my hips are by far the sexiest, most feminine things about me.

Do all the good you can and create a life that feels good on the inside, not one that just looks good on the outside. It is inner beauty which matters most.

—DR. ANIL KUMAR SINHA

Learning to love my body has really helped me avoid all the competition and cattiness that unfortunately permeates Los Angeles and especially *Shahs of Sunset*. And it's definitely helped me stay grounded and confident while under the pressure of being on TV. When the first season of *Shahs of Sunset* aired, it felt like walking into that classroom in Germany all over again. I was being scrutinized and judged in all the same ways, and it shook my confidence to the core.

Most people on TV have a certain look that is very polished and put together. They fall into one category or another and are carbon copies of each other instead of true originals. We're so used to this that we assume viewers will only want to look at physically perfect people. I am a real person who is far from perfect. In order to fit into one of those existing categories, I would have had to lose weight, tame my hair, and use contouring makeup to make it look like I had a nose job.

Realizing this, I found all my old insecurities rearing their ugly heads. Reza and I were the only two people on the show with our original Persian noses. Maybe my nose *was* too big, after all. It was a huge struggle to stay true to myself, but if I changed what was rare about me, I wouldn't be rare anymore. I'd be common. Ordinary. *Nah*, who wants that? I've never had a small nose, and I have never in my life been a thin girl, so why would I strive to make myself something that I am not? I knew that at the end of the day, if they wanted me to be on the show, they'd want the real me. And that's exactly what they got.

But it didn't stop there. As soon as we started filming, both GG and MJ started talking all kinds of garbage about my body and my looks in general. They said I was fat and ugly, that I looked like a transvestite, that my thighs were covered in cottage cheese, and on and on and on. It was not easy to sit there and listen to all this nonsense being said about me publicly and not either get angry or start believing that what they were saying was true. In fact, it was one of the hardest things I've ever done. But I knew I had to walk my talk, and I relied on my rituals more heavily than ever to keep my confidence up during this time.

Looking at those girls, I saw clearly that they were just projecting their own self-hatred onto me. They'd already changed all of the things that had once made them unique in an effort to look more "normal" or stereotypically beautiful. But all those changes happened on the outside. They'd never gone within and done the work to let go of those insecurities and learn to love themselves. So when they saw their own original features on me, they projected all of their internalized self-loathing onto me and attacked.

Then there are the viewers who think that just because you're in the public eye, they have the right to publicly voice their opinion about you, no matter how rude or hateful that opinion may be. To this day, when I post a picture of myself on Instagram, for every positive and loving comment, like "I love your style" or "You're such a natural beauty," someone will inevitably comment that I look fat or that I need a nose job. It's almost enough to throw me back into my old negative thought patterns and start thinking that maybe I should lose weight or get a nose job to make myself "worthy" of being on TV.

It's only by connecting to my Inner Priestess through my beauty rituals that I'm able to remember that I'm already worthy. Looking like someone else won't make me any better or more valuable. The people who make these negative comments are just directing all of their own baggage and insecurities at me. If I changed one thing about myself to please them, they'd only go on to attack another. It never ends. The only person I can aim to please is me, and I can only do that by loving and accepting myself.

PRIESTESS POWER POINT: BEAUTY ATTRACTS BEAUTY

It may sound strange to you, but surrounding yourself with beautiful things, especially ones from nature, will actually make you feel more beautiful. Try placing a single flower next to your bed so it's the first thing you see when you wake up in the morning. This simple practice will connect you to nature and allow you to harness your own natural beauty.

Next try taking this a step further and placing flowers on your desk, at your table, or wherever you'll see them throughout the day. These don't have to be expensive. Cheap flowers from the corner market will do just fine! If flowers don't do it for you, that's cool. Find something that *you* think is beautiful. Don't knock it until you've tried it, lover. Remember, anything that works is a go. Don't judge yourself. Just do what works and revel in the results.

If you find yourself cutting down other women or feeling competitive, take a moment to think about where that negativity and judgment are really stemming from. Do you have a bad habit of criticizing other people for the same things you dislike about yourself? When you learn to love and accept yourself and believe that you are enough, you'll stop competing and looking down on others. Instead, you'll want to celebrate what makes them unique, too. This newfound compassion and positivity will make you that much more beautiful from the inside out.

The rituals below have helped me learn to love and accept myself while constantly working to improve. Striving to make yourself better doesn't mean you're not good enough already. Self-improvement is something that is never complete. You are good enough right now in this moment, but you can always get better. There are eternal steps you can take to become the very best, most beautiful, loving, compassionate, sexy, and fierce version of you. I hope these tools help you move forward on your path of connecting to and unleashing all the power of your Inner Priestess. *Salamati!*

For beautiful eyes, look for the good in others; for beautiful lips, speak only words of kindness; and for poise, walk with the knowledge that you are never alone.

—AUDREY HEPBURN

⤌⟐ BEAUTY BATH RITUAL ⟐⤍

<u>You'll need</u>: rose oil, bathtub, candles (optional), loofah, and a full-length mirror

<u>Time allotted</u>: 30 minutes, at least once a week

This sacred ritual will help you literally and figuratively wash away all of your negative feelings about your body and find the sexy self-confidence that is the real you. I suggest doing this once a week at a time that you plan in advance. No half-assing this at the last minute, babe. In order for this to work, you have to really commit and plan to do it at a time when you can invest all of your energy into getting into the zone and being fully present. I like to think of my rituals as part moving meditation, part performance. By that I mean that you must show up for yourself and focus on becoming fully conscious and aware of your every breath, every movement, and every thought.

The other key ingredient to making this work is the belief that it will. If you complete this ritual with your guard up or your eyes rolling back into your head, you're not giving yourself a chance to really connect. I know it can be scary as hell to tear that wall down and tune into your heart, especially if it's been a while since you've done that, but it's the only way you're going to move forward. If you don't already feel amazing about yourself, you need a paradigm shift, and you can't grow unless you're willing to change. As you prepare for the ritual, notice the doubt set in, but don't attach to it. That doubt is not a part of you. I promise you can do this, and it will be beyond worth it.

Step 1—Prepare

Take care of your inner, spiritual beauty. That will reflect in
your face.

—DOLORES DEL RÍO

Show up for your beauty ritual at the appointed time. Make
sure you have at least thirty minutes to dedicate to the practice so you won't feel rushed and that you have some space to
yourself so you can do it in private. Try to find a time when
your roommate, family, or boyfriend is out of the house and you
have total peace and quiet. Make sure that nothing and no one
will distract you. Turn off the TV, and definitely turn off your
phone. Nothing is more important right now than dedicating
this time and space to yourself. Get ready to turn it all the way
on like you would for a big performance. This is your chance to
show up big for yourself and make things happen!

Now, take a moment to transition from all the other activities
you did today to your ritual. First, shake out your body to release
any stress or tension that you're holding on to. When you're ready,
sit still and take a few deep breaths. Dim the lights if you like or
close your eyes, consciously slowing down your thoughts as you
begin to focus one hundred percent on the task at hand.

As you breathe, don't worry about forcing yourself to erase
your negative thoughts. It's natural for those to pop up again
and again, and consciously trying to get rid of them is coun-
terproductive because it gives them too much power. Instead,
allow yourself to become aware of your thoughts and to watch
them pass by like clouds. Some of those clouds will be white

and fluffy. Others will be dark rain clouds. Don't judge them or yourself either way. Your thoughts are not who you are. Just let yourself enjoy watching the parade of clouds go by.

After tuning in and watching your thoughts for a few minutes, you'll sense when you're in the right frame of mind to begin the ritual. It's when you feel your thoughts slowly fading and your intuition kicking all the way on. You may suddenly feel happier and more powerful. That's because your Inner Priestess has entered the room. Once you're in that space, do everything you can to stay there. Keep your energy focused, your breath steady, and your mind soft. Continue to let your thoughts float by without any judgments or attachment.

Step 2—The Bath

Something with inner beauty will live forever, like the scent of a rose.

–ALEX FLINN, *BEASTLY*

Slowly and mindfully move into the bathroom if you're not in there already. Dim the lights and light some candles if you want, and run yourself a nice warm bath. Once the tub is full, put three drops of pure rose oil into the water. The use of scent is an important part of this ritual. As you come to associate the smell of rose oil with this ritual, your mind will naturally focus on the beautiful scent of the rose oil instead of any passing thoughts or distractions.

Just as the smell of food prepares your body to eat by starting your digestive system, the scent of the rose oil will prepare your mind and body for the coming ritual. I like to use rose oil because it helps me feel deeply connected to my childhood in Iran and it's an ancient, sensual scent. If you have an aversion to the rose oil, you can try using lavender essential oil instead.

As you step into the bath, focus on all of your senses. What does the water feel like on your skin? What does your foot look like when it is submerged? Pay attention. What do you hear? How does the rose oil smell? What does it remind you of? Now slip all the way into the bath, immersing yourself up to your neck. Close your eyes and lie still in the water, breathing in the rose oil and remaining aware of your body. What thoughts are coming up for you now? Don't fixate on them, just be present and observe. Try to relax all of the muscles in your body, especially your facial muscles and your jaw. Release any tension you're holding on to. It's not serving you right now.

Continue to focus on your breath as you bring awareness to every part of your body. Starting with your toes and working your way up to your neck, consciously feel the water embracing you one body part at a time. If you practice yoga, this may remind you of the final relaxation pose, or Shavasana, while the bathwater and rose oil add a lovely sensual element to this sacred tradition. Continue to let your thoughts pass by unjudged as you feel yourself letting go and melting deeper and deeper into the water.

Step 3—Visualization Exercise

Outer beauty is a gift. Inner beauty is an accomplishment.

−RANDI G. FINE

After bringing awareness to every part of your body, it's time to begin your visualization. With love and compassion in your heart, think of all the ways you criticize your body and all the parts of you that you fear aren't enough. In great detail, imagine every one of those imperfections being washed away by the water.

Really work to see it in your mind's eye. If you think you're too fat, picture every ounce of that fat being stripped away from you as if it's dirt on your skin. If you think your thighs are too big or your ass is too flat, see them coming off of you. Don't stop until you've imagined every part of you that you feel insecure about coming off and rinsing right down the drain.

Now open your eyes. Take a loofah or another exfoliator and very slowly go over every part of your body, one at a time. As you go over each body part, imagine yourself gently and compassionately wiping away any negative thoughts you have about it. Start with your right foot and work your way up to your neck, skipping nothing. If you think your toes are ugly, wipe that thought away. If you believe your thighs are too big, wipe that thought away. If your belly is flabby or scarred, wipe it away. If your breasts are too big, too small, or too droopy, wipe those thoughts away. You have the power to cleanse yourself of every last negative thought and feeling about your body. Take your time with this. There's nowhere else you have to be.

When you've gone over every single part of your body, put the loofah down and take a few moments to gently wipe your hands over your face. Start at your chin and caress your face with your fingers and then your palms. Now stroke your hair, brushing it away from your face. Do this a few times. Most of us never think to touch our own face and hair, but it's so important to be affectionate with yourself. Sensually caress your face and hair. This is the skin you'll walk around in throughout your entire life. It does everything for you, and if you disconnect from your body and beat up on it with negative thoughts, you'll never feel truly confident. Mindfully touching your own skin reconnects your body and mind. They are one and the same.

When you're done, take a moment and feel the difference in your body now that you've wiped away all of your negative thoughts. Visualize those thoughts as being separate from you. Do an honest assessment here. If you don't feel like you've washed everything away, pick the loofah back up and start over again. Don't step out of the bath until you feel completely cleansed.

When you're ready, get out of the bath and imagine being reborn, like a butterfly breaking out of its cocoon. Not one of your judgments or self-critiques is coming out of the bath with you. You're leaving that all behind. It's only your golden Inner Priestess who's stepping out of the tub. This is your chance to start over, and any negative thoughts you have from now on are something you are creating brand new. The old judgments— your deepest insecurities, the parts you thought weren't good enough, and the names people called you in school—are gone. Only your gorgeous, clean, purest self remains.

Step 4—Mantra

Inner beauty, too, needs occasionally to be told it's beautiful.

–ROBERT BRAULT

Dry yourself off, and then step in front of a full-length mirror completely naked from head to toe. Don't pose or vamp here. No one is watching but you. Set a timer and stand there for at least three full minutes looking at yourself in the mirror. Now, here's the thing, babe—the monkey is going to start rattling his cage, especially the first few times you do this. If you expect this to happen, it won't be so hard.

Your mind is most likely going to fill with negative, judgmental thoughts about yourself. *My stomach is so big. My boobs are sagging. My legs are covered in cellulite. My face looks old. My skin is pale.* It may be a long list. Whatever you do, don't deny these thoughts. Observe them like you did in the bath. They are merely clouds in the sky. It may feel like you're at war, being bombarded with self-criticism, but if you force yourself to withstand it, I promise those thoughts will eventually fade. You're strong; you can take it.

The reason this is happening is that we've awoken the beast with this ritual. The only way to slay the dragon of your critical self once and for all is to allow her to rise up instead of stuffing down those negative thoughts because they're too painful. Now we can see her fully in all her glory. She's not so scary, is she? This dragon—your critical self—is not you. You're free to observe what she thinks without attaching to it at all. It's very powerful to stare her in the eye and finally be fully aware of your deepest insecurities. Often we overcompensate for these self-criticisms by building our egos up around them, and it's important to shed those layers. As these thoughts come up, release ownership of them. They are allowed to be there. They are not you.

After the three minutes are up, or when these thoughts begin to slow down, look yourself in the eyes and say out loud, "I am enough just the way I am. I am beautiful." Repeat this three times while looking in the mirror. You may feel silly talking to yourself at first, but stick with it and you'll feel stronger and more confident each time you say it. When you're done, you'll feel a radiant sense of peace come over you. Take a breath and enjoy that feeling—you earned it.

What you do next depends on what time of day it is. If you're going to get ready for bed, put on your favorite pajamas. This can be a sexy nightie, a pair of silk pajamas, or whatever makes you feel the most beautiful and radiant. Climb right into bed, and you should sleep more peacefully than you have in a long time.

If it's not bedtime yet, take some time to put on one of your favorite outfits. I do this even if I'm not planning to go out afterward. My favorite outfit to go dancing in is a huge flamenco skirt with a crop top, tons of bangles, gold earrings, and Nikes so I can really enjoy dancing. This outfit makes me just as happy when I put it on to dance around in my bedroom!

Dressing up just for myself after completing this ritual pushes my confidence over the top. Put on your favorite music—for me, it has to be Prince, Sade, or Michael Jackson. There's very little those lovers can't help me heal. Enjoy playing dress-up like you did when you were a kid. Have fun; no one is judging you! If you do go out afterward, you will exude a brand-new sexy confidence that is the real you. Enjoy this powerful feeling and see what happens when you start to live with this energy radiating from you at every moment. I hope it's as life changing for you as it has been for me.

Our hearts are drunk with a beauty our eyes could never see.
–GEORGE W. RUSSELL

Mini Beauty Rituals

While you indulge in your beauty bath once a week (or more if you have time), there are several rituals you can practice in between that will boost your confidence in just a few minutes. Try to do at least one of these every day to make yourself feel gorgeous and alive. After trying them all, you'll see which ones have the greatest impact and focus on those. While the beauty bath is a deep and sacred ritual that requires a lot of focus and attention, these are meant to be nothing but fun! Let loose and enjoy honoring yourself and your unique beauty.

PRIESTESS POWER SHOWER

This is a great alternative to the beauty bath if you don't have a bathtub, you're short on time, or you want to enhance the results of your practice. I recommend doing this at least once or twice a week in between doing the full ritual. It's especially powerful to do this one before getting ready to go out, as it'll help you ooze sexy confidence wherever you go.

To do this, get in the shower, and as the water is coming down over your body, visualize it washing away all of your negative thoughts about yourself. Just as you did in the bath, picture them in great detail coming off your body and rinsing right down the drain. Feel free to add the rose oil to the shower just as you did in the bath if you enjoyed that part of the ritual. When you step out of the shower, you'll feel like you're glowing. Now stand naked in front of the mirror and just smile as any negative thoughts pop up. The more you do this, fewer self-critiques will arise because you'll wash more and more of them away.

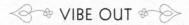

⊰ ✦ VIBE OUT ✦ ⊱

This is a simple and really fun way of connecting to your Inner Priestess to boost your confidence before going out or whenever your soul needs a little pick-me-up. Try this the next time you go on a date or before a romantic night with your beloved! To do this, put on one of your favorite outfits, play your favorite music, and throw a dance party just for you. When you're feeling down, music changes everything, and dancing shifts your energy. You know the saying "Dance like no one's watching"? That's what I want you to do here. Bust out those favorite dance moves and go ahead and sing along.

I always "vibe out" while getting ready to go out. I put on some music, do my hair, lovingly put on all my gold jewelry, and sing and dance around while I'm getting dressed and putting on my makeup. It's my special "me time" that I often look forward to and have more fun doing than actually going out! Sometimes I have so much fun that I don't even bother going out afterward, but when I do, I know that my inner joy and confidence are coming with me.

SNAP A #SELFLOVESELFIE

I am the first to admit that the world of selfies is ridiculous. They're all about showing off artificial, airbrushed images of perfection instead of revealing the real you. A #SelfLoveSelfie is different. This type of selfie is all about being real, accepting yourself, and celebrating your golden inner beauty.

To express true confidence, start posting pictures of yourself on social media that make you feel gorgeous instead of the ones you think other people will like. There are endless apps to alter your pics and make you look like someone else, but the point here is to avoid all that and post a pic that shows your true beauty. It may take fifty pictures to find the right one, but so what? Part of the fun is the process of honoring yourself with your own little photo shoot.

To create a #SelfLoveSelfie, put on an outfit that makes you feel amazing, play around with your makeup, and then start shooting away. To get the best angle, hold the phone about a foot above your head and angle it down toward you so you're taking the picture from above. Then turn your face to the right and the left to find the right light. In your mind, repeat the affirmation from the beauty bath as you snap away: "I am enough just the way I am. I am beautiful." Keeping this thought in your mind as you take the pictures will cause the golden light of self-love to shine through your eyes.

The more often you practice these rituals, the more fun and effortless they will become. You'll have fewer negative thoughts, and instead your heart, mind, and soul will be filled with a pure joy, love, and gratitude that can't be bought or faked and that are truly *ziba*, beautiful. *Boos*, lover!

Nothing can dim the light which shines from within.

–MAYA ANGELOU

chapter four

ATTRACT YOUR SOUL MATE

Your task is not to seek for love, but merely to seek and find all the barriers within yourself that you have built against it.

—RUMI

PRIESTESS PREVIEW

In this chapter, you'll learn how to complete the following rituals:

✦ Get Your Vibe Up

✦ Heal from the Past

✦ Shoot Out Your Love Energy

Whether you are in a relationship, married, or single, these rituals will help you connect to your one and only beloved and attract the exact type of sacred relationship you want.

The rituals in this chapter are some of the most powerful ones in this book, and I am so excited to share them with you. Don't you dare skip this chapter if you're already in a relationship and think you don't need it! Whether you are single, dating, or married, there is always more work to be done to create a strong, healthy, beautiful, and passionate relationship.

So often, we obsess about finding someone when we're single, and then once we get into a relationship, we stop thinking about it and start focusing on other areas of our lives. *Nah, nah, nah.* Once you have found your soul mate, it's even more important to nurture that relationship and make sure you never take it for granted. A soul mate is a precious, rare thing that must be cherished.

Yes, I absolutely believe in soul mates and that every single one of us has one. I define a soul mate as someone whom you have a deep and profound connection with. Someone you love unconditionally and who makes you feel completely comfortable and at home.

But here's the thing—you can't feel at home with someone else until you feel at home with yourself. If you're walking around every day feeling depressed, unhappy, or just generally unsatisfied because you're waiting to meet your soul mate, it will never happen.

Sorry if that sounds harsh, babe, but it's the truth. This is because like attracts like. Any vibration will attract a similar vibration, and the closer the vibrational match, the stronger the magnetic pull. This means that the frequency you're putting out into the world is being pulled back toward you. If you're single and constantly meeting the wrong guys (or girls), it's time to think about what sort of vibrations you're putting out. Why are you attracting these people?

If you're in a relationship that's not going as well as you'd like, it could be for the same reason. A lot of people talk about how relationships (especially marriage) require work—and I agree—but I take a slightly different approach. Instead of working on the relationship itself, your relationship will benefit even more from work you do on *yourself*. If you're not a hundred percent happy with your relationship all the time (and, seriously, who is?), the only way to make it better is to make *yourself* better. Any negative vibrations that you're putting out will damage your relationship and your chances of attracting your soul mate—even if you're not aware of it.

Being deeply loved by someone gives you strength, while loving someone deeply gives you courage.

—LAO TZU

⟜❦ STEP 1—GET YOUR VIBE UP ❦⟞

The vibrations you're sending out into the world are a direct reflection of the chatter in your head. The negative chatter in our heads about relationships is so damaging. We live in our heads. The game is won in your mind. What we think is in so many ways what we are. If you want to attract your soul mate, you must turn off this negative chatter. Remember during the Priestess Detox how you learned to focus in on the chime and ignore the noisy horns? You must do the same thing when it comes to your thoughts about relationships.

Again, this is often as simple as flipping the script from thinking about what you don't have to focusing on what you do have—or even what you'd like to have. I see so many single ladies obsessing about being alone. They can't sleep because they're thinking about how badly they want to find love. They can't enjoy social events because they're so embarrassed to show up alone. If you do this, it's keeping you energetically in a place of lack. That is not a place that attracts love, and this line of thought will never allow your soul mate to come into your life.

A lot of girls who are in relationships also block love from coming to them by doing virtually the same thing! Instead of being grateful for what they have and what is going right in their relationship, they are focused on what is going wrong in the relationship—what is lacking. But this very energy will prevent things from ever getting better!

I'm not saying that you should just ignore major problems if your relationship isn't working out. Of course not! After completing the Priestess Detox, you probably already have a good idea of whether or not your relationship is salvageable. What I'm saying is that if you love this person and want things to work out, you need to focus your energy on the good things about your relationship and stop the negativity and nit-picking.

If he or she is cheating, lying, or treating you wrong, you know what you need to do. But if he or she just leaves dirty socks on the floor, doesn't make as much money as you'd like, or wears the same hideous sneakers all weekend long, tune those things out and focus your energy on listening for the chime. What do you love about this person? What is he or she doing right? Those things are so much more important than the imperfect or annoying ones.

It's time for a major energy shift. No more desperation, negativity, or loneliness—whether you're in a relationship or not! Think again about the fact that like attracts like. That means that if you want to attract love, passion, and sensuality into your life, you need to live in a place of love, passion, and sensuality. Before you can attract your soul mate, you have to become your own soul mate. You have to get your energy up to a frequency that matches the way it feels when you're in love. This is how you'll attract that very love into your life.

Think about that exciting time when you first meet some-one. You jump out of bed in the morning, eager to embrace the day. You sing in the shower. You're excited about life. You're in a mystical, blissful, sensual, meditative state. That is what it means to have a high frequency, and with that vibration, you'll attract more of that exact same thing to you. The rituals in this chapter will help you raise your frequency and become full of peace and joy and inner beauty so that you become a magnet for a loving, romantic, and soulful relationship. Love won't be able to resist you.

But how can you get your vibe up so you can become your own soul mate first? Sometimes you have to fake feeling good in order to change your energy. This is not about putting on an act, but rather amplifying what is good and abundant in your life instead of focusing on what is lacking. If you love your job, throw your energy into rocking it at work even more than usual. If you have a great group of girlfriends, plan an extra-fun girls' night out. If you've been wanting to learn a new skill or try a new hobby, now's the time to go for it. Stretch yourself. Indulge yourself. Love yourself.

All along, listen for the chime, and work on balancing out your internal voice. If you feel yourself sinking into a negative vibration, practice the gratitude ritual from the Priestess Detox every night before bed. And do anything and everything you can to make your days feel beautiful and sensual. Dress in something that makes you feel good, even if it's just to go to work or to the grocery store. Treat yourself to fresh flowers. Indulge in a massage. Do whatever makes you feel amazing and complete. Your soul mate can only arrive when you are at home and in love with yourself.

If you find yourself feeling resistant while reading this and doubting whether there really is anyone out there for you, I want you to know I feel you. I have nothing but love for even my most cynical lovers! But here's the thing, babe—manifesting your soul mate requires trust and belief. That's because love itself requires those two things. You can't fully love someone without trusting him or her, can you? So how will you ever be able to manifest your soul mate without believing that it's possible?

Your cynicism may feel like it's an important part of who you are, but it's exactly what's blocking you from love. And you're the only one who's suffering. If you're an analytical person, it may be hard to let go and just trust. I understand that. But anything having to do with love and sensuality requires throwing out that analytical mind and living straight from the heart.

The fact that you're reading this book is a clear sign that you want to live a life of happiness and fulfillment. Yet you're still blocking your own happiness by holding on to your doubts. I'm not trying to change who you are. You can be supercynical, and maybe your soul mate is cynical, too! But you'll never find that person until you let go of your doubts and fears and get your vibe up. Then you can enjoy going back to being cynical together.

Love has reasons which reason cannot understand.
—BLAISE PASCAL

The story of my beloved and me illustrates how I was able to find my soul mate when my vibe was way up.

When I moved from Germany to Beverly Hills in 1991, I was in tenth grade. My English was okay, and for once I looked like the other kids around me, but I was clearly still an outsider. I dressed different, acted different, and thought differently than the people around me.

This was possibly the hardest time of my life. After years in Germany, my father had been able to open a small corner store that sold Mediterranean food. We finally had our own house and things were going well for our family. But we still couldn't escape from the ugliness around us.

At this time, there was a lot of racism in Europe. A huge number of Turkish refugees had settled in Germany, and the Germans blamed them for stealing their jobs and their opportunities. Because we were refugees with brown skin, people assumed we were Turkish, too. I remember being pushed on the street by an old lady who cursed at me in German. My mother faced discrimination when looking for work. And then the Berlin Wall fell, and our family faced another political upheaval.

Skinheads set a fire in my dad's store, broke the windows, and painted swastikas on the walls. This happened not once but three separate times. It wasn't safe there. I couldn't believe that we were being forced out of our home yet again, but it was too risky to stay, and my family sought refuge in LA.

My father, my brother, and I all left for Los Angeles, while my mother stayed in Germany for six months to settle our affairs. Those six months were so hard for me. I was in a foreign land again, and this time without my mother. I knew how much my father and brother missed her, too, and I felt that I needed to act as daughter, sister, and mother to them. Meanwhile, I was thrust into the very strange new world of Beverly Hills High School.

By that time, I thought of myself as a badass poet, artist, and activist. I was really into music, style, art, and politics. But when it came to guys, I was supershy. I guess I was a bit of a late bloomer when it came to dating and relationships. In Germany, some of my friends were really promiscuous at a young age, but that was never my style. Even then, it was important for me to have a connection with someone first. I never dated. And someone I liked always started as a friend first.

During my first month at Beverly High, I was hanging out on the big lawn in front of the school. I gazed across the lawn and suddenly locked eyes with a guy I'd never seen before. Jermaine. Though I'd already been in the States for a few weeks, his was one of the first faces I remember seeing in America. Out of nowhere, I felt an incredibly intense connection and chemistry, and just like that, I knew.

We smiled at each other from across the field. From that moment on, our eyes would meet every time we saw each other. We'd smile at each other and stare into each other's eyes, but we never actually met. And I thought of him fondly throughout the rest of my high school years as our connection continued, but I didn't feel any urgency or possessiveness about him. I wasn't thinking, *I need to be with him*. I simply enjoyed the feeling of our soul connection. I let it be, knowing that the universe had its own plan for me.

Twenty years passed. I traveled to India. Jermaine moved to New York. I thought about him from time to time with a smile, and I often wondered what he was up to. But during this time I was really focused on raising my frequency. I had bought and renovated my own home (more on that later!), grown as an artist, and developed my rituals. I was at home with myself and living a high-frequency, sensual, and loving life. I was so grateful for everything I had accomplished.

Then in 2010, it was my mom's birthday weekend. Her sisters were visiting from Germany, and we had a huge barbecue at my parents' house. With my cousins and aunts and uncles there, it felt as fun and festive as the picnics and birthday parties we shared as kids. I was having so much fun that I didn't even mind that my phone battery had died—even though I was shooting the first scenes of *Shahs of Sunset* the next day and my phone had been blowing up all weekend.

My cousin Seti told me that she wanted to walk to the Grove, which is a big, gorgeous outdoor mall in Los Angeles. It's at least a half-hour walk from my parents' house, but this is what we Persians like to do—eat and then take long walks in big groups. I was tired, and I told Seti that I was going to take a nap while they went for their walk, but she begged me to come with them. "You can charge your phone at the Apple Store," she told me.

"Okay, fine," I relented, and off we went—thirty Persians walking and talking loudly as we made our way to the Grove. When we got there, I went into the Apple Store and plugged in my phone. When it finally turned on, I started scrolling through my messages. By then, it was early evening. The sun was just starting to set and the sky was a gorgeous shade of blue.

As I was standing there reading my messages, a strange yet very peaceful feeling came over me. I picked up my head and looked toward the door. It was as if a magnet was pulling my eyes toward the entrance to the store. A beautiful man walked in, and I felt something I had never experienced before. It felt like a magical, mystical waterfall washing down my soul. The chemistry between us was so strong.

I immediately looked away. The connection I'd just felt was too much—it overwhelmed me. I guess I was still sort of shy when it came to guys! I looked back down at my phone, and within seconds I could feel him standing right behind me. I gathered my strength and looked up, and suddenly, I was looking directly into those eyes again. It seemed like no time had passed. Our eyes locked. "Asa?" he said, and I knew for sure that it was Jermaine.

We were both filled with joy as we smiled and laughed and began to catch up with each other. The energy between us was so pure and innocent, like the energy between children. It was timeless. By the time we separated with plans to see each other again soon, I was completely breathless and yet full of life.

I rejoined the rest of my family (who immediately began making fun of me), and within five minutes we bumped into Jermaine again as we made our way around the Grove. This time, it felt like seeing a man I'd been in a relationship with for forty years. He met my whole family and fit in right away. My brother, Arta, and Jermaine had been in gym class together back in high school, so they immediately started catching up. Soon, they were reminiscing and cracking up about old stories. This added another level of awesomeness to everything I was experiencing. I was mystified, intrigued, and yet completely at peace. I was home. And Jermaine and I have been inseparable ever since.

Love is composed of a single soul inhabiting two bodies.

—ARISTOTLE

PRIESTESS POWER POINT: CREATE A SACRED LOVE ALTAR

No matter what your relationship status is, a powerful way to let God or the universe know that you are serious about attracting love into your life is to create a love altar in your home. This is a sacred space that's dedicated to your soul mate and your relationship with him or her—whether that relationship is a part of your life now or will be in the future.

To do this, choose a quiet and peaceful place in your home. Ideally this should be in a corner of your bedroom—somewhere safe and private. Have fun creating this space! You are going to spend some time sitting there as you do all of the rituals in this chapter, so you might want to add a pretty floor cushion to sit on, a table that's low to the ground, or just a simple piece of fabric that marks the space as sacred and separates it from the rest of the room. Two things I highly recommend adding—on the table or on the floor—are a candle and a fresh flower.

The flower can come straight from your garden or the grocery store. It does not have to be expensive. But you should replace it regularly to keep your love altar alive. Any time you spend nurturing this space will help you draw your soul mate closer to you and bring you closer to yourself. I've always been an internal astronaut, exploring my own galaxy within. Your soul mate altar is the perfect place for you to do that.

The more you go within, the more powerful and strong you'll grow. It can be difficult to explore your weaknesses along with your strengths, but the more you do, the more energy you'll radiate to attract all of the things in life that are yours, including and especially your soul mate. When you spend time at this altar you are endorsing yourself, telling the universe that you are special enough to take a moment for yourself and that you are worthy of a soul mate who will treat you with the same loving care and attention that you show yourself.

STEP 2—HEAL FROM THE PAST

We're meant to learn and grow from relationships, but most of us don't take the time to make sure we're spiritually ready before jumping into a new relationship, with baggage and hang-ups piled on top of our spirits. We go into that new relationship in worse shape than we were in before, which is the opposite of how it should be.

Every relationship you go through should make you stronger, teach you things, and ultimately bring you closer to yourself. This is how you will prepare to meet your soul mate. But so many of us are so afraid of being alone that we don't take the time to heal and learn from our relationships when they end. We step right into a new one, and then we're shocked when that one falls apart, too.

Babe, the reason your relationships are not working is that you haven't let go of the baggage from your past. This may be the case even if you're in a relationship or a marriage right now. Even if you aren't aware of it, you might have insecurities and fears from the past that are affecting your relationship today.

Have you been cheated on in the past and now you have trouble trusting your man? Or did you cheat in the past and now you secretly blame yourself for the end of a relationship? It's easy to see how these examples might be impacting your relationships, but even baggage that's not quite as heavy can do the same thing. Just like you had to wipe the slate clean during the Priestess Detox to prepare yourself for everything you want in life, you must, must, must let go of past relationship baggage in order to attract your soul mate.

The weak can never forgive. Forgiveness is the attribute of the strong.

–GANDHI

Soul Mate Ritual 1—Letting Go of the Past
<u>You'll need</u>: journal or paper, pen, candle, metal tray
<u>Time allotted</u>: 30 minutes, just once—more as needed!

No matter how old you are or how many relationships you've been in, baggage from past relationships may be holding you back from your soul mate. The same thing holds true even if you're in a relationship. This baggage might be keeping you from sharing true happiness with your beloved. It's time to stop aligning yourself with damaged energy of the past. Whatever happened in the past helped you become the fierce lover you are today.

It's hard to see this sometimes. A relationship ends, and we put on damaged emotional weight that keeps good energy away. We attract more and more negative energy, and eventually we grow bitter. That's the kiss of death when it comes to attracting your soul mate. You can't fill yourself up with love and fulfillment if you're already full of insecurity, fear, and baggage. Just like you did during the Priestess Detox, it's time to empty your vessel so you can fill it back up with positivity.

Each of us has two voices—the one that we speak with out of our mouths and the one we speak to the universe with through our energy. You may tell your friends that you are ready for a new relationship, but if you're still thinking about what your old boyfriend did to you, you're telling the universe the exact opposite truth. This inconsistency will keep your soul mate away. It's crucial to balance these two voices and get your energy as ready as your mind for your soul mate. That's what this ritual will help you do.

Gather your things and go to your soul mate altar. Take a few deep breaths and shake out your body. Then light your candle. Close your eyes and take a moment to think about your past relationships. If you've had several serious relationships, think about them one by one. As you think about them, let all of your regrets about these relationships come up in your mind.

They will probably come in the form of all the ways you think you've failed. *I was too selfish. I was too clingy. I was too critical.* Just let these thoughts appear and observe them. A lot will come up at first, and then they'll slowly start to dissipate.

Once your mind has calmed down, open your eyes. On your paper or in your journal, write down all of the things you did to keep the relationship from flourishing. It doesn't matter if these things actually caused the relationship to end or not. They are the things you are holding on to, the sources of guilt and regret that are blocking you from fully moving on.

As you write each one down, offer it to the fire. Yes, I mean that literally. Burn the piece of paper in the flame of the candle. Even burning it just a little bit on the end will do. If you aren't comfortable burning things, imagine yourself offering all of your failures to a fire. One by one let them catch fire and go up in flames. Really see the paper burning in your mind until nothing is left of it.

When you are done offering your failures to the fire (either literally or metaphorically), close your eyes and take a moment to feel the difference in your body. Those failures are gone now. They are not a part of you anymore and cannot affect your relationship with yourself or your soul mate.

If you complete this ritual and still feel like there is baggage from the past weighing you down, repeat the self-mythology ritual on page 36. It's possible that you are holding yourself back not because you blame yourself or your failures, but because you are blaming your former partner's failures.

Remember, you are not a victim in this life. You are in control. No one has the power to stop you from getting everything in this world that is yours, especially your soul mate. When you take your life into your own hands, you will create the space for him or her to enter.

If you are in a relationship now, it's important to do a second step to this ritual, which is offering to the fire all of the ways you've failed in your current relationship. Are you taking your boyfriend or husband for granted? Are you too stubborn or selfish? Or do you flirt with that cute coworker in a way you know your man wouldn't like?

Close your eyes again and let these thoughts come up. None of us is perfect. We all make mistakes in every single one of our relationships. The important thing is to let them go before they overpower the things you're doing right. Write down each of the ways you've failed in your current relationship and offer them to the fire. They are not a part of this relationship anymore. You are free to move on without the burden of guilt about anything you've done wrong.

Love is life. And if you miss love, you miss life.

—LEO BUSCAGLIA

Soul Mate Ritual 2—Express Gratitude for the Future

<u>You'll need</u>: journal or paper, pen, small box

<u>Time allotted</u>: 30 minutes

Now that you are free of your baggage from the past, it's time to move on and start attracting your soul mate to you.

You've emptied yourself of negative feelings, and you can fill yourself back up with positive feelings about what you want for the future, whether you're in a relationship or not.

So many of us are particular about the little things in our lives—what we eat, what we wear, what type of TV we own, even our specific coffee order—but we spend so little time focusing on what we want in our soul mates. When you're working on attracting your soul mate, it's incredibly important to know exactly what you are trying to attract. You need to be able to see and visualize what your soul mate is like before you can attract him or her to you.

Sit at your soul mate altar and close your eyes. Imagine your soul mate. What is he or she like—tall, athletic, smart, intellectual, funny, or serious? Come on, don't just picture Ryan Gosling and call it a day. Think of specific qualities you want in a soul mate. What kind of person do you want to be with? What do you want to do together? What do you want your lives to be like?

When you can really picture it, open your eyes and write down a list of the qualities your soul mate possesses. Don't be embarrassed—no one has to see this but you! Write down what your soul mate looks like, acts like, and dresses like. Is he or she kind, educated, close to his or her family, sarcastic, silly, shy, or gregarious? Write down as many details as you can. This is like putting in your order with the universe. But instead of ordering a thin-crust pizza with extra mushrooms and jalapeños (yum!), you're ordering your soul mate. Make sure to be specific so you don't get the wrong order.

If you're already in a relationship, instead of writing down what you want in a soul mate, write down a list of what you appreciate in your partner. This is a great way of showing gratitude for having a soul mate in your life. What do you love about this person? Is he a great dad? Does he take care of you? Does he make you laugh or make you think about things in a new way? Write it all down.

Finding your soul mate is something to be thankful for, but the journey isn't over once he or she is in your life. Instead, this is where the real dance begins, and it's much more of an active process than most people realize. In fact, I'd say that most relationships end because people stop proactively working to make things better. When you're with someone for a long time, it's so easy to forget all the things you loved about that person to begin with and instead obsess about the things that bother you about them.

My parents are the perfect example of this. They've been married for forty-five years and have obviously been through a lot together. After surviving war and raising two children, my mom still hates it when my dad eats sunflower seeds and leaves the shells on the floor and gets superannoyed by the noise he makes when he cracks them. Sure, these things are annoying, but we all do annoying things. Just like we all have negative thoughts. Instead of letting those things bother us, we have to listen for the chime.

Forget the sunflower seeds; what are the things your soul mate does right? Taking a moment to express gratitude by writing down everything you love about your soul mate will keep you in a place of gratitude that allows love to flourish. It will keep your energy way up there as a couple. I can't tell you enough how important this is! Being in a relationship is sacred. You have chosen this person to fly with among everyone in the entire world. There's nothing more sacred than that. Never forget that!

Stop and take a moment to express your gratitude when he makes you laugh, when you see him give your daughter a hug, or when he makes your coffee the way you like it without you even having to ask. Gratitude feeds the flame in a relationship, and when you stop feeding the flame, it dies. Carry that candle from your soul mate altar with you, and light that flame in your heart with gratitude as often as you can.

You can give without loving, but you can never love without giving.

–ROBERT LOUIS STEVENSON

MINI SOUL MATE RITUAL— SHOOT OUT YOUR LOVE ENERGY

This short but powerful miniritual will work alongside the two main rituals in this chapter to help draw your soul mate to you or keep the flame alive if you're already in a relationship. Practice this every night before bed to keep yourself in a warm, sensual state of high-energy, high-frequency love.

Every night before bed, take a moment for yourself. Go to your soul mate altar and light the candle. For just a moment stop the world and focus on your soul mate. Wherever he or she is, picture your soul mate in your mind and greet him or her. Close your eyes. Visualize shooting all of your love and energy out of your heart and all the way to the end of the universe. It will reach your soul mate, whether he or she is in your house or halfway across the world and whether he or she is in your life right now or not.

It doesn't matter whether you had a terrible day, you feel desperately lonely, or you just had a nasty fight with your boyfriend. Take this moment for yourself. Smile as you close your eyes and shoot out your heart energy to meet your soul mate. Doing this every night before bed will raise your vibration and make you a magnet for everything you most want. And you deserve every last bit of it.

True love is eternal, infinite, and always like itself. It is equal and pure, without violent demonstrations: it is seen with white hairs and is always young in the heart.

—HONORÉ DE BALZAC

chapter five

HONOR
YOUR FAMILY

We are born of love; Love is our mother.

—RUMI

PRIESTESS PREVIEW

In this chapter, you'll learn how to connect with your ancestors, identify and release the triggers that bring up all of your family baggage, and create your own meaningful family rituals. These steps will make you feel deeply connected not only to the people who came before you, but also to the golden priestess inside of you.

When I was growing up, my family was very close. I'm not just talking about my nuclear family, though we were close, too. I mean my huge, loud, beautiful, crazy extended family that included my grandparents, aunts, uncles, and dozens of cousins who were all around my age. We all got together every weekend. If we weren't picnicking by the water, we were playing games, cooking and eating enormous amounts of delicious food, putting on shows, and holding dance contests.

My mom was often in the kitchen with my aunties drinking tea while my dad played games with us kids. He was (and still is) the best dad—a fun and energetic uncle to my cousins and a loving, kind father to my brother and me. When my cousins and I went swimming, he chased us, pretending to be a shark, and when we held huge dance contests, he was the judge. Somehow, he made us all feel like the winner. When we go on vacation together, my dad still pretends to be the shark, and I'm forty years old! It cracks me up to this day.

My parents and my brother were my foundation, and my cousins filled in the rest of my world. All of my childhood memories include them. We played together, ate together, often slept together at each other's houses, and dreamed about the future together.

One of my clearest memories as a child was lying on the floor of my bedroom with my cousin Goli. We took turns imagining where we'd be in the year 2000. Back then, the new millennium seemed so far away, almost as if it would never actually arrive. I wish I could remember what I said when it was my turn to predict where I'd be in the year 2000. I'm pretty sure I got it completely wrong. I never could have guessed that I'd be where I am today!

Those years were the best and the worst at the same time. Despite the war and our uncertainty about the future, I felt safe nestled in the warmth of my loving family. I felt at home. And then, of course, we left Iran and everything that was familiar to us. I never saw my grandparents again. When they died, my family wasn't able to attend their funerals or even visit their graves because it was too dangerous for us to step foot in our own country. It's been more than thirty years since we left, and we still haven't gone back to Iran.

One of the hardest things about moving to Germany was missing my cousins. It was like being in a new world without my arms and legs. I had to adapt to this strange foreign place without these essential pieces of myself. Eventually, a few of my aunts and uncles and cousins joined my family in Germany, but many of them stayed in Iran, where we couldn't visit them. They're still there today. And we ended up leaving Germany just a few years after we arrived there. Once again, I had to adapt to life in a new world without my appendages.

My mother didn't see her own sister, Fereshteh, or her daughters, Goli and Yalda—my cousins—again until more than

Golden Gate Park at the end of a California road trip,
San Francisco, 2002.

On one of my art
adventures in LA
where I would drive
around the city and
take pictures. For
many years I always
had my camera
around my neck and
a Polaroid and journal
in my purse. This
was during my mega
corset phase, 2004.

My super-handsome Baba Joon, aka "Mashti," in his navy uniform, Abadan, Iran, 1970.

My Disco Priestess uniform: a big ruffled flamenco skirt, a gold-beaded fringe top, and Nikes for *serious* dancing the night away, Beverly Hills, 2002.

⤳✤ CONNECT TO YOUR ANCESTORS ✤⤳

You may be thinking, *Well, I grew up in the same town I was born in and have always lived near my family, so I can skip this part. Vaysa!* Keep reading. Even if you grew up surrounded by family, it's still important to honor your ancestors. How can you ever expect to feel connected to yourself if you don't honor the people who created you? Every single one of us has a unique ancestry going back thousands of years. Your lineage includes many thousands of different people, many of whom you've never met. Each of them has their own unique story, and without just one of them, you wouldn't be you. Think about how amazing that is!

Most of these people are already gone, but if you never think of them and let them be forgotten, you are missing out on connecting to a deep, important part of yourself. Your history is a part of you. It sculpted and created that gorgeous Inner Priestess whom you have inside of you. Connecting to your ancestors and honoring your history are two crucial parts of uncovering your Inner Priestess.

Where did your ancestors come from? What were their lives like? A lot of my confidence has come from knowing about the exact part of Iran that I'm from and connecting to its culture. My mother is Sumerian. She was born in the state of Khuzestan in southern Iran. The Sumerians were the first urban civilization in southern Mesopotamia. Some experts believe it was the first civilization in the world.

The people from that part of Iran are Afro-Iranian and have their own culture and heritage that's completely different thirty years later, when we managed to plan a family reunion in Turkey. You may have seen some of this reunion on Season 3 of *Shahs of Sunset*. By then, our lives were so different from when we left Iran. We were grown women. My cousins had babies of their own! It was so wonderful to see them again, but it was also a painful reminder of how much we'd missed out on. We never got to see each other grow up. I couldn't attend my cousins' weddings or throw them a baby shower or just simply be a part of their lives. My mother missed out on thirty years with her sister. And after that brief reunion, they returned to Iran while we went back to Los Angeles. Who knows when we'll see them again?

Growing up disconnected from my country and my extended family left an enormous hole in my heart. I became what I refer to as emotionally homeless. I always had a place to live, but I was unrooted from my homeland. If you unroot a tree, it cannot survive, but I wouldn't let this happen to me. To fill the hole in my heart and feel more grounded, I began practicing rituals that helped me connect to my extended family and even the ancestors who came before us. Of course, these rituals were actually connecting me to my Inner Priestess and myself.

A happy family is but an earlier heaven.
—GEORGE BERNARD SHAW

Shooting an art video in Joshua Tree. The morning after a beautiful full moon art adventure in the desert, 2006.

Arta and I having fun at the beach, one of our favorite places.
Baby Priestess as always, voguing, Bandar Anzali, Iran, 1981.

My absolute favorite picture of my Mami Joon and Arta.
LOVE them, Ahwaz, Iran, 1976.

Chahar shanbe soori—fire-jumping ritual for the ancient Persian new year Nowruz with Baba Joon. Cleansing yourself of the negative of the old year and purifying for the new year to come, Bandar Anzali, 1981.

Arta and I playing in the garden. I always had "healthy thighs" as my mom would say, Abadan, 1979.

Arta and I in front of our beach house. I'm voguing again, Bandar Anzali, 1980.

Mami Joon, Arta, and me, Abadan, 1977.

My parents happily dancing at their garden wedding. She wore a powder yellow dress and he wore a powder blue suit, Ahwaz, 1973.

My beautiful Queen, Mami Joon, at my grandmother's house, Ahwaz, 1975.

Me in my room stylin' and profilin'. Frizzy hair and brows phase before moving to the United States and discovering coconut oil, Hamburg, Germany, 1990.

Our very first year as refugees in Germany. Hard times, but small things made us happy, Hamburg, 1984.

My super-cool Baba Joon, who owned the very first record player in Mashad. He used to take it everywhere with him, even to outdoor picnics, Mashad, Iran, 1962.

Teenage Priestess. This was my very last day in Germany before we moved to LA. I was vibing to the max, wearing my mom's seventies wrap skirt as a cape, a Persian tablecloth as a skirt over black biker shorts and black nylons, a Nike T-shirt, and, of course, Jordans, Hamburg, summer 1991.

learn about your past. We are so lucky to live in a time when we have access to this information. Take advantage of it!

Once you are more educated about your ancestors, begin to incorporate their culture into your life more and more. This can be as simple as putting up a painting in your home, listening to music from your culture, or trying a traditional recipe. You'll find that it feels good to do this. It's fun! There are so many different paths on the journey of self-discovery, and this is an important step.

LET GO OF YOUR BAGGAGE

Once you have begun to connect to your ancestors, it's essential to honor the people who brought you into this world and gave you life—your parents.

No matter how much you love your parents, it's very likely that you are carrying around baggage from your childhood that's still affecting every part of your life today. It also may be preventing you from being as close as you'd like to your parents. You may already know very well what these issues are, but there may be some messages you received as a child that are affecting you now without you even realizing it. Either way, it's critical that you decode your family baggage and make peace with the past.

No matter how perfect or traumatic your childhood may have been, we all have issues stemming from the way we were raised. That's because we identified with the messages we received as children. Without realizing it, we internalized these messages and they became a core part of who we are.

from the rest of Iran. It's a very ancient part of the world, and I feel deeply connected to those roots. My mother feels this way, too. She and her sisters returned there to give birth to their children, no matter where they were living at the time.

Knowing that my ancestors and I were all born in this same ancient place is very meaningful to me. When I listen to Khuzestani music or eat seafood, which is more popular there than in the rest of Iran, my soul feels at home. (Yes, lover, that's why I'm so obsessed with ceviche!) It awakens the ancient DNA inside of me. I incorporate elements of that culture into my life in every way I can to stay awake and energized. All of my gold jewelry designs are based on ancient Persian designs, and I have pieces of art and artifacts all over my house that represent my heritage. When these things surround me I feel more empowered than ever to be completely and fully me.

You can do this no matter where your ancestors are from. Every culture has its own rituals, art, food, and music. If you're not already familiar with your culture, begin to explore it. View this as more of an ongoing exploration than a onetime ritual. Connecting to your ancestors isn't something you can do once and then move on and forget about it. Get to know the place your ancestors are from, whether it's another country, another state, or just another town. If you were born in the same town your ancestors came from, delve deep into your town's history— I bet you'll learn some amazing things you didn't already know about your local history.

If you don't know where your ancestors came from, there are great at-home DNA kits available now that can help you

If you were told as a child that you were the "pretty one" and your sister was the "smart one," you may still believe that you have nothing to offer the world except for your looks. This can have an impact on what jobs and opportunities you go after, what dreams you pursue, and even what relationships you get involved in. If you were abused or neglected as a child, you may identify with not deserving real love. Or maybe you identify with your family's problems and have taken them on as your own.

The truth is that none of that crap is who you are—not your parents' problems, not the things they told you about yourself, and not the ways you grew up feeling inferior or less than. Babe, if you don't believe me, think about all of the messages I received as a child. In Germany, I faced constant racism and bullying. People on the street called me *Ausländer*, which means foreigner in German. Should I have taken that on as part of my identity? Do those words define me? *Nah*. Of course not. Just as the messages you received as a child have nothing to do with you. You are your Inner Priestess— that pure being who existed before you received any messages about who you were and who you weren't. It's time to get back to being her.

A family is a place where principles are hammered and honed on the anvil of everyday living.

—CHARLES R. SWINDOLL

IDENTIFY YOUR TRIGGERS

When I lost my land and became a refugee, my parents became my land. They are my roots, and they are everything to me. Ever since my family started appearing on *Shahs of Sunset*, fans love to talk to me about my relationship with my family. They often tell me about their own families—how they've grown apart or lost their parents, and how much regret they have about all the things they didn't say and do before that happened. This regret leads to guilt, and so often it eats these people alive. It's hard to move forward or grow when you're filled with guilt and regret.

It hurts me to hear this. Hearing all of these stories has made me even more grateful for the relationship I have with my family. We're extremely close. We spend most of our free time together, and ever since I launched my company, Asa Kaftans, we've also been working together! They have been a part of the company from day one and are still my most trusted and valuable employees. We have our share of arguments, but nothing is more important than the love and respect we have for each other.

I am so grateful for this. But it hasn't always been this way. As you read earlier, I used to have a lot of resentment about the fact that I grew up without a role model in business. I never saw anyone in my family being tough and ruthless, and I thought I would never have the skills I needed to succeed in that world. Even then, I realized that this was pretty minor compared to all the things that some parents fail to give their kids. But the point is—no parent is perfect. They are human, and they all fail their children in some large or small way.

Before I learned to let go of my family's baggage, I could feel it weighing me down and keeping me from enjoying my time with them and my relationships with other people. This didn't start until we moved to America. In Iran, our lives were so different from what they are now. The world my parents came from was so safe and familiar. They were surrounded by people they'd known their whole lives. They socialized with family members. And they learned to only see the best in people. There was no reason for them to see anything else.

Sure, there was local gossip and small dramas, but my parents did their best to stay out of all that. I saw plenty of harshness in Iran during the war and later in Germany, but not any ruthlessness or competition between individuals. I wasn't aware of that part of life until we were in America. As soon as we moved to Los Angeles, I saw how hard it was to make it in this country and realized there were some people who would stab you in the back if you trusted them.

That's when I started to wonder how my parents were going to make it in this world. But no matter how much their environment changed, they stayed the same. They were good and kind and continued to see the best in people, even those who would hurt them. They were selfless, and suddenly the people around them were eager to take advantage of this.

At the same time, I was hyperaware of everything my parents had given up for me. They had sacrificed their whole lives so that I would get a chance to have a better one. When I was in high school my parents slept on a futon in the living room, worked two jobs, and never complained, but my mom always looked so tired. In America, she never looked as carefree as she did back in Iran. She was a working mother in Iran, too, and I'm sure she was also tired back then! But it was different. Escaping from Iran and then building our lives up again from scratch twice had taken a huge toll on her.

I knew that my parents had given up everything for my brother and me and that they were suffering every day. They had changed their lives so drastically for us, and I put a tremendous amount of pressure on myself to become successful in order to make their sacrifice worthwhile. But even as I did become more successful, it still felt like it wasn't enough. My parents had given up way more than just their material things to give me my freedom. They had given up their families, their comfort, and their happiness. No matter what I did, it didn't feel like it was enough. What would it take to make their sacrifices worth it?

Let me be clear—my parents never did or said anything to make me feel this way. They never once made me feel guilty for everything they'd done for me or implied that I owed them anything. I'm sure they didn't see it that way at all. But I already knew that I had an inner strength, and I realized that maybe I could help them. While they were suffering, I was thriving. The survivor in me had come out to party, and I knew that I could thrive in any situation. I was determined to use this ability to make their lives better.

In America, I had found a way to fit in while being true to myself. I made new friends, my style was fresh, and I had a great time listening to music and having fun. I decided that I was going to take matters into my own hands and make things amazing for my entire family. I knew it would take a while (and I'm still working on it!), but I was motivated to stop relying on my parents and let them rely on me instead.

I'm an Aries fire dragon (yes, lover!) and very action oriented and violently solution oriented. My parents are the opposite. One of the things I constantly worried about was my parents' inability to take action. When little things came up they put them off and said they'd look into them tomorrow. But tomorrow never came. That inaction became my trigger. It drove me crazy, and it led to fight after fight after fight with the people I loved the most in this world.

Does this sound familiar? We all have triggers when it comes to our families, and it's incredibly important to get to the root of them so you can stop reacting to them with anger and resentment. It took me a long time to figure out why my parents' inaction was such a trigger for me, but I finally realized that it stemmed from the same core issue as my resentment about their lack of business savvy. At the end of the day, I was worried about them. I didn't want them to get taken advantage of, to get hurt, or to find themselves in over their heads because they didn't take action to solve a simple problem. I wanted their lives to be easy.

If this had been a friend or even a boyfriend, maybe I would have just stepped out of the relationship. But my parents are a part of me. Their issues are my issues, and I knew that unless I changed something, nothing would improve. Constantly fighting with my parents about their unsolved problems was getting me nowhere. I had to change the dynamic.

Once I recognized the pattern that had been triggering me, I realized that I had to separate myself from my parents' negative patterns. Inactivity was a problem for *them*, not me. This sounds so simple, but it's actually really hard to do. When you've spent your entire life being triggered by something, it is incredibly difficult—and ultimately liberating—to say, "This is not my problem."

You may think you've already separated yourself from your parents' patterns by going in the other direction. Let's say your parents were hoarders. Growing up, your house was full of junk, and you've separated yourself from this negative pattern by virtually never buying or keeping material things. On the one hand, you've changed the pattern. But on the other hand, you're still reacting to the way you were raised instead of finding your own path that's totally and uniquely yours.

Going to the opposite extreme may seem like a step in the right direction, but it still gives the original pattern too much power. It's actually not that different from just repeating the same old pattern! The trick is to separate yourself from the pattern completely so you can be the real you.

Insanity runs in my family. It practically gallops.
—CARY GRANT, *ARSENIC AND OLD LACE*

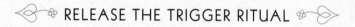 RELEASE THE TRIGGER RITUAL

<u>You'll need</u>: journal or paper and pen
<u>Time allotted</u>: 30 minutes

Step 1—Discover Your Trigger

As with so many things, the first and most important step here is awareness. When you start looking at your life with honesty, it's not that difficult to let go of your baggage. But you can't let it go until you know what it is and how it's holding you back.

Have you ever noticed that when you're with your family you sort of revert back to the age when you were the most angry and confrontational? For most people, that's their teen years. This is so common that it's almost a cliché to talk about acting like a teenager when you're with your parents. But have you ever wondered why this happens? It's not just because that's the age you were when you last lived together. It's because when you are with your parents, you are constantly being triggered by the same negative patterns that have created all of your baggage. When you are triggered, you get angry, and you can't help but act like a bratty teenager!

If you're anything like me, you then feel really guilty for lashing out at your parents. This makes family reunions unpleasant for everyone. But there is a way to stop this nasty cycle. It starts with recognizing your trigger points. When you start paying attention, you'll realize that it's the same few things that are always triggering you. In most families, there are probably two or three triggers that cause the majority of fights and conflicts.

These fights might manifest a little differently each time, but the triggers at the root of them are basically the same.

Take your journal to a quiet and peaceful spot. Close your eyes, and think back to the last three arguments you had with your parents. It doesn't matter whether you just got a little snippy with them or whether they snowballed into a huge battle—any disagreement is fine. One by one, go through each of the last conflicts and answer the following questions. This is going to require you to take an honest look at your own behavior, so remember not to judge yourself too harshly when answering these questions. This is not about making you feel guilty for how you reacted! The answers lie in those reactions, though, so you have to look at them before you can figure out how to stop yourself from reacting that way ever again.

1. What happened?

Describe the argument. Who said what? How did it start? Where did the argument lead? How did you leave things?

2. How did it make you feel?

Were you hurt, angry, or something else? What specifically did the other person say to make you feel this way? How did you react to feeling this way?

3. Why do you think you felt this way?

Take a moment to think the situation through again. Why did you *really* get upset? What was triggered inside of you that made you react?

After you answer these questions for all three of your last arguments, read them over, looking for any overlap between them. I'm pretty sure it won't be hard to find. The issue that made you react each time is your trigger. These triggers represent the negative patterns in your family. They are deeply rooted and color every interaction you have with them. Once you know what these patterns are, you are halfway to ending them for good.

If you still can't figure out what your triggers are, don't worry. Sometimes we have more than one trigger or we have one that isn't so easy to uncover. As you move forward, start paying close attention to any feelings of resentment or anger toward your family. Every time you feel this way, go back and answer these three questions. I'm sure that before long, you'll be able to identify your triggers and move forward toward taking away their power.

If you do have a sense of what your triggers are, take a moment to write them down. These can be bullets, sentences, or full paragraphs—whatever feels natural to you. Here's an example from my journal.

My triggers are:
When my parents put off taking action
When my parents are overly kind and generous to strangers
When my parents sacrifice their own needs for the needs of
other people

The family is one of nature's masterpieces.
–GEORGE SANTAYANA

Step 2—Release Your Trigger

No matter what your parents did (or didn't do) to create this trigger, remember that they tried their best to be good parents to you. Our generation is so much more emotionally analytical and in tune with these dynamics than our parents. They rarely thought about things like patterns and triggers—they were just trying to get through the day and put food on the table! And as they were doing that, they never took the time to identify their own triggers and the patterns they inherited from their parents. And what about their parents? They never separated themselves from their parents' patterns, either. And on it goes, all the way up your family tree. Some of these issues have probably been in your family for many generations.

But guess what, babe? You have the power to end this negative pattern once and for all—not only for you, but also for the sake of your children and your children's children and your children's children's children! Think about all of the people you'll be helping by taking the time to put a stop to this negativity once and for all.

Close your eyes and think about your grandparents on both sides of your family. What were they like? What were their biggest challenges and obstacles? For many of us, our grandparents grew up in a time when they had to fight every day for their survival because of war, poverty, or the Great Depression. What did this do to them?

Now picture your mom and dad as children. What was their relationship with their parents (your grandparents) like? If you don't know the answers or never had a chance to get to know your grandparents, take some time to ask your parents about them. The more you learn about your parents' childhoods, the more you'll understand where their issues and limitations stem from.

What you're really doing here is finding compassion for your parents. When you do this, the trigger starts to lose its power because you see that it has nothing to do with you. It's not your problem; it's theirs.

This happened for me when I realized that my parents' inactivity had nothing to do with me. It was actually my boy Reza who first helped me see this. We were talking about my childhood and how my parents escaped from Iran when he asked me, "Do you know how much strength they must have had to get you out of that situation?" I paused for a moment, intrigued. I had never thought about it that way before. "Babe," Reza continued, "your parents are thugs."

This was a huge lightbulb moment for me. I already knew that everything my parents had gone through was crazy. It was the kind of stuff that could ruin someone for life. I was keenly aware of how much my parents had sacrificed for me, but I never realized how strong they had to be in order to do it.

I realized that maybe this was why they were so passive and slow to take action in their lives now. No one can be a warrior 24/7, and they had used so much strength just getting us to Germany and then to America. That's when it hit me. For years, I'd believed that I was strong and they weren't, so I had to take care of them. But suddenly I realized that I was strong because they were strong. I had gotten all of my strength from them.

This realization changed everything for me. I still felt responsible for my parents, but the resentment I was holding on to about their inaction melted away. Taking care of my parents is no longer something I felt pressured to do—it became a joy. It is now one of the greatest joys of my life.

My dream now is to have a huge compound where my entire family and I live together in superclose proximity. Of course, all of my friends think this is a terrible idea. Working with my family is nuts. I'm my parents' boss, and we get on one another's nerves a thousand times a day. But we still spend more time laughing together than we do yelling at one another. We have fun together. And being with them is not a sacrifice at all. Nothing about our relationship is perfect, but it is real, and I love it. And now that their kindness and generosity no longer trigger me, I can see that these are the same traits that make my parents so easy and fun to be around. Ironically, they're now the things I love most about them!

Go back to your list of triggers and read them over one by one. Then close your eyes and repeat to yourself, "This is no longer a trigger for me." Do this every day if you have to! You are taking back the power to control your own life. You do not need to be triggered by these patterns any longer. It feels good to release these triggers because it sets you free. You can do anything without this baggage holding you down.

Here's another example of how this worked in my own family. In our culture, the Persian New Year (Nowruz) is a huge deal. It has been celebrated on the first day of spring for more than three thousand years. It's like Christmas and New Year's in one. Plus, it always lands right around my birthday, which adds a special significance for me.

There are many ancient rituals associated with Nowruz. Persians prepare for the holiday by doing a major spring-cleaning of their house. In fact, lover, this may be where the whole concept of spring-cleaning originated! We also buy new clothes to wear on the holiday. As you may have seen on *Shahs*, another Nowruz ritual is to make a bonfire and jump over it while saying *"zardi ye man az to, sorkhi ye to az man."* This means "My yellow is yours, your red is mine." In other words, you are asking the fire to take your sickness and problems and replace them with the fire's warmth and energy. It is a way of purifying the soul before the start of the New Year.

In my family, we always celebrate Nowruz with a big party at my parents' house. Every year Mom goes crazy hosting because she wants everything to be absolutely perfect. She loses her mind. First, she takes three weeks off beforehand to prepare. She spends weeks shopping for hundreds of ingredients and cooking literally dozens and dozens of different dishes. Whatever you're picturing right now, double it. Seriously, babe, you're *still* probably underestimating the amount of work she does. It's insane.

A few years ago, my mom was working so hard to prepare for Nowruz that she collapsed on the kitchen floor. We had to take her to the emergency room. She was fine (thank goodness!), but she's so stubborn that she got right back to work. When I saw her working so hard, I got so upset because I was worried about her. I didn't think she could keep going like this.

My fear about her overdoing it and having no boundaries with what she does for other people triggered me, and it led to fight after fight between us.

Just a couple of years later, my mom was working so hard that she had to go to the emergency room again. Her knee also started to swell up from spending weeks on her feet chopping herbs and preparing food. She just has no limits when it comes to giving to others. This selflessness was another trigger for me, and I found myself jumping at her when I saw her doing this. Then we'd argue. It was a predictable pattern that we played out time and time again.

Finally, after completing these rituals I realized a few things that really helped me change this dynamic. First, I realized why my mom's crazy cooking habits were triggering me—I was afraid that she wasn't strong enough. I remembered what Reza had said. She was strong enough to escape from Iran and then Germany to provide a safer life for my brother and me. She's stronger than I gave her credit for. And beyond that, it's futile to try to change her. She is who she is, and her selflessness is one of the things I love most about her. If she wants to bust up her knees cooking like a crazy person, that's her problem—not mine.

Now, when I see my mom going crazy on Nowruz, I roll my eyes and jump in to help her instead of jumping *at* her. I don't criticize her or try to change her mind, and now we don't fight. This allows us to enjoy the holiday and our time together, which I realize is all that my mother really wants, anyway. Releasing the power of this trigger has helped me give that to her. And that's a great feeling.

Whatever else is unsure in this stinking dunghill of a world a
mother's love is not.

— JAMES JOYCE, *A PORTRAIT OF THE ARTIST AS A
YOUNG MAN*

Step 3—Express Gratitude

Like I said earlier, no parents on this whole planet are perfect.
Maybe your dad left when you were little. Maybe your mom
always criticized you. Or maybe your parents were loving and
kind but they weren't the exact type of parents that you thought
you needed. No matter what they did right and what they did
wrong, your parents did one thing perfectly—they brought you
into this world. They created you. That is sacred.

Your mother carried you inside her womb for nine months
and then went through labor to birth you. Even if they failed
you from the moment you were born, you owe your parents your
respect and gratitude for giving you the amazing gift of your
unique and precious life.

Even more important, you owe it to yourself to forgive your
parents for whatever they did wrong, for however they failed
you, and for anything they didn't give you—no matter how badly
you may have needed or wanted it. Any resentment, anger, or
negative emotions about your parents that you're holding on to
are just weighing you down. They're not hurting your parents.
They're hurting you. You want to rise up, grow, and evolve, but

you can't do it with negative emotions pulling you down. You have to release them in order to thrive.

Your relationship with your family may not seem that important to you, especially if you're not that close or live far away from one another, but your family dynamic still has the power to change your entire life. If there's bad blood between you and your family, it can affect your whole being for the rest of your life. It's not like a bad breakup that you can move on from. It is a part of you forever.

It's so easy to get caught up in what your parents didn't do. Maybe they didn't pay for you to go to college. Maybe they did more for your sister than they did for you. Or maybe they even gave you up for adoption and you're holding on to anger toward them for not taking care of you. I'm not dismissing any of that. These feelings are real and justified. But lover, you have to realize that this anger and resentment is only hurting you—and only you have the power to release it.

Whatever they did wrong and however they failed, your parents played a huge role in getting you this far. Beautiful, magical circumstances needed to come together for you to become a part of this world. Your parents were the lead players in this amazing symphony. The way they met and the feelings they shared are all a special part of that. They may have done everything wrong as parents, but they had the magic formula to make you. That's enough. They don't owe you anything beyond the life they gave you.

We all naturally look up to our parents, but they aren't superhuman. They're just regular people doing their best to make their lives work in a tough world. And they have their own baggage from their childhoods to deal with. Despite all of that, they made you perfectly. That is something to be thankful for, and showing gratitude to your parents for giving you life is exactly how you'll take your power back. What your parents gave you is sacred. Sorry, babe, but you're not allowed to keep having negative feelings about that.

Close your eyes and silently express thanks to your parents. Repeat to yourself, *Thank you for bringing me into this world and for helping me get this far.*

If your parents are no longer with you, it's still important to express your thanks to them. Whether you had five minutes, five years, or fifty years together, that time was sacred and you should be grateful for it. It's a gift to spend time with the people who created you. Close your eyes and repeat to yourself, *Thank you for the time we had together.*

It's also important for you to let go of any guilt you're feeling about not spending enough time with your parents or not appreciating them when they were here. That guilt is not serving you. Let it go. You did your best. Deep down, your parents knew that, and they loved you—that's for sure. You don't need to carry this baggage with you any further into your future life. You are free.

You don't choose your family. They are God's gift to you, as you are to them.

—DESMOND TUTU

CREATE A FAMILY RITUAL

The final step to taking control over your relationship with your family is to work on creating rituals that you can share with one another for years to come. You probably already have some rituals in your family, and I'm guessing they involve food. I love how every major religion has a sacred ritual around food. Jewish families share Shabbat dinner every Friday night. Christians eat a big lunch after going to church together on Sundays. And Muslims often eat lunch together after a Friday-afternoon prayer service. Breaking bread together is sacred, and you can make it a special family ritual whether or not you ascribe to any particular religion.

In my family, our ritual was always a Sunday barbecue. My dad is a total barbecue master, and no matter where we lived, he always found a little spot outside to set up his multiple grills. When we first moved to America, my parents were always working, but no matter how busy or exhausted they were, they always found time for our Sunday barbecue. It was nonnegotiable, and no matter what else was going on, we always made time for it.

I clung to this tradition. It made me feel so safe and nurtured despite all of the change we'd been through. Every week, we sat together talking and eating the same foods we ate back home. I remember feeling so connected to one another and to our homeland. Even as a teenager who mostly wanted to go hang out with her friends, I looked forward to our family dinners every Sunday.

Every dinner was a group effort. My dad did the barbecuing, my mom prepared the meat, and I helped her make the salad as my brother put out the dishes. As we got ready, we talked and joked with one another. It was our way of getting back in touch with one another after the long, busy week.

I recently found a picture of my family and me when we were living in Germany. We had our Sunday barbecues then, too. But there it was much more difficult. The weather was cold and dreary, and we lived in a tiny storeroom with no place for a grill. That didn't stop us. We took the subway an hour each way to a park in Hamburg, each of us carrying a thousand things—two separate grills, huge pots of food, multiple salads and other side dishes, hot tea, watermelon, knives, and glass teacups. Once we got to the park, we set up our barbecue in the dead of winter. All of a sudden, it started to snow. But we didn't care. We joyfully ate our meal right there in the freezing cold as the snow landed softly on our plates of food.

It was amazing to look at that picture of my family eating a huge meal off real plates in the snow, knowing that we had to travel an hour back home by subway carrying all of that stuff with us. I was struck by how badass we were. Nothing, and I mean nothing, was going to keep us from our family ritual. We were so dedicated to being together. Those memories are precious to me now, and I'm so grateful to my parents for making that ritual nonnegotiable.

Take the time to slow down and prioritize the things in your life that really matter. Spending time with your family is surely one of them. If your family lives far away or you don't have any family, substitute the word "family" for anyone that's really important to you. Your family is your tribe, whether that's your parents, cousins, your own children and partner, or your friends.

Who are the positive forces in your life whom you want to make time for? Start a weekly meal ritual with those people. It can be as simple as pasta night with your roommates. Just make a meal and sit down with the people you love. That's the ritual. Cooking the meal yourself will keep you connected to your food and to the entire experience. It doesn't have to be gourmet or perfect. Try a new recipe together and get everyone involved. If it comes out terrible, you'll laugh about it for years to come. And those memories will be delicious, nurturing food for your soul.

The family—that dear octopus from whose tentacles we never quite escape, nor, in our inmost hearts, ever quite wish to.

—DODIE SMITH, *DEAR OCTOPUS*

chapter six

TURN YOUR HOME
INTO YOUR HAVEN

It may be that the satisfaction I need depends on my going away,

so that when I've gone and come back, I'll find it at home.

—RUMI

PRIESTESS PREVIEW

The rituals in this chapter will help you clear the clutter from your home and redecorate with intention so that your home evokes the exact sensation you want to feel every time you step inside. Your home will become your haven, a paradise that brings you confidence, peace, and joy every day of your life.

My memories of Iran are slowly fading. So much time has passed since I've been there. Now, when I think of Iran, all I can conjure is a certain feeling. It's not a specific memory or any particular moment. It's the way the air felt when I breathed it in. The smell of jasmine and roses. The safe, comforting, and unmistakable feeling of *home*.

The Farsi word for garden, *pairidaeza*, translates into the English word "paradise." That should give you a good idea about how we Persians feel about our homes. We have ancient, deeply rooted rituals and philosophies about the home. Huge gates separate the homes in Iran from the rest of the world both literally and energetically. Entering the home is like leaving one world behind and entering a completely different universe.

Traditionally, extended families in Iran live together, so the home is where our whole tribe gathers. We spend a lot of time at home. It's an indoor-outdoor campus where we live, eat, sleep, and play. Outside, there are fig trees, fountains, flowers, and plants. Inside, there are ancient artifacts and simple, well-chosen decorations.

In Iran, hosting is a big part of our lives. Guests are seen as a blessing, and when you walk into someone's home, they treat you like a king or queen. We practice specific rituals and ceremonies to symbolize unity, joy, and family. When my family lived in Iran, we were already a modern family. Instead of a gated estate, we lived in a nice condo. But through our customs and rituals, we re-created the feeling of a traditional Persian home.

They didn't live with us, but all of my cousins lived nearby, and we spent all of our free time together. My home was their home, and we spent countless hours playing together in the garden while our mothers were in the kitchen and our fathers played cards nearby. With my whole extended family there with me, there was no reason to go anywhere else. It really was *pairidaeza*.

In Germany, our home was a far cry from the paradise I grew up in. It was a tiny storeroom that was dingy, dark, and musty. The first time we entered that space, I watched in awe as my mother calmly got out a big bunch of esphand, a traditional Persian herb that is used to ward off evil spirits and bad energy, and lit it with a match. She slowly walked around the small room, burning the esphand as the smoke swirled its way into every corner, nook, and cranny.

Of course, I'd seen my mother do this many times before. Even before we left Iran, my family moved a lot because of my dad's position in the navy. We went with him wherever he was stationed. Every time my family entered a new home, I watched my mom burn sage or esphand to cleanse the energy in the house. Then she lit candles and displayed some of our most prized possessions to make us feel at home. But the energy in that storeroom seemed so helpless and beyond repair. I was surprised that my mother would bother to cleanse the energy even there.

Watching her, I learned two valuable lessons at the same time. First, I realized with a sinking feeling that this really was our new home. It was nothing like the condo we lived in back home or any of the homes we'd lived in before. But this was suddenly our new reality. I had no choice but to accept it. At the same time, I learned that no space is truly beyond repair. If you approach it with intention, you can create your own paradise even in the darkest of places.

And my family did create our own little paradise both in that storeroom and then in the run-down apartment we moved to in Beverly Hills. We used our love and energy to make each space our own. There, we laughed together, played together, and shut out the rest of the world with an energetic gate instead of a literal one. It was enough to sustain me through those hard times and make me feel at home.

Ironically, losing my home twice and starting over in new and increasingly foreign places made me feel more connected to the idea of home instead of less. While I learned the value of letting go of material things that didn't matter, I became even more attached to the true treasures that I brought with me from one continent to another. At the same time, I learned how to create the *feeling* of home anywhere at anytime.

It's that feeling that my friends and family immediately pick up on when they walk into my house. You might have seen this happen on *Shahs of Sunset*. When people enter my home, they instantly feel welcomed and at peace. They want to take their shoes off, relax, and have a cup of tea. My home is a haven for my friends and family. It's a place where we can escape from the stress of the world and truly enjoy being together.

Do you think this happened by accident? No, lover—
nothing this good in life happens that way! I created every
detail of my home with intention, from the foundation to the
furniture. I was extremely fortunate to be able to buy my own
home back in 2003. It was a little beach cottage, and I had the
honor of doing a lot of construction on it myself. I knew this
was my chance to create something really special from the very
beginning, so I was extremely involved in every aspect of planning and building it from the ground up. I wanted the house we
were building to feel completely and uniquely mine.

Before we poured the foundation, I wondered what I could
do to bless the house and make it really special. Of course, I
thought back to my home in Iran. The first thing that came to
my mind was the smell of roses—in particular, the roses in Iran
that have such a deep fuchsia color that they are called Muhammad's blood roses. They have a unique smell that permeated my
childhood and an ancient beauty that I wanted to carry with me
into my future. I wanted those ancient vibes from my culture in
my home, so I put petals from Muhammad's blood roses in the
foundation of my house.

The next thing that came to my mind was, of course, gold.
Gold is not only a huge part of my culture, but it also saved
my life when my family escaped Iran. Gold is magical to me.
I wanted gold and everything it symbolizes to be a part of my
home, so I buried thirty thousand dollars' worth of gold coins in
the foundation right near the front door of my house. This was
my way of wishing luck and wealth to everyone who entered
my home.

I know this is pretty extreme. Maybe I really am a "vierdo"! But, hey, I'm Persian. A little superstition never hurt anyone. The construction guys thought I was insane. They just wanted to lay the darn foundation already. There was just one guy on the team who seemed to really get what I was doing. We had a long conversation about our cultures, and he explained to me why corn was so important in his culture and the ancient culture of the land we were standing on.

As proud as I am of my Persian culture, I am also very proud to be American, and I wanted to honor the land my home stood on, which is sacred Native American land. Right before they poured the foundation, I added native corn to the rose petals and gold coins to bless the earth.

I didn't stop there. After the house was built, I chose every item that went inside with extreme attention to detail. If something was going to find a home inside of my home, it had to make me feel good or remind me of who I am. I lovingly found places for my vinyl collection and my favorite books that have inspired me. I continued the Persian custom of putting a big mirror near the entry of my home so that if anyone comes in with bad intentions, they'll be reflected back onto them. (Like I said, a little superstition never hurt anyone!)

Near the front of my house where I knew I would walk past them every day I placed pictures of my grandparents. In his picture, my grandfather is sitting in a field in the south of Iran holding a *Tasbih*, which are Persian prayer beads. The picture is a little bit overexposed, and he looks so comfortable and peaceful, almost tribal. In her picture, my grandmother is standing in

front of an ancient mud house in Iran wearing a veil. She was
the only woman in my family who always chose to wear a veil,
and wearing it, she looks serene and beautiful. These pictures
bring up strong emotions every time I look at them. They make
me feel a deep sense of peace and connection to my culture, my
heritage, and ultimately myself.

If you go anywhere, even paradise, you will miss your home.
—MALALA YOUSAFZAI

I decorated my entire house with this level of intention,
constantly asking myself, *How do I want to feel when I enter this
room?* I put up an energetic gate around my home. When I
come home from the outside world, I take a shower and change
into clothes that I wear just at home. I never wear shoes in my
home. These are my small ways of respecting my home space
and protecting it—and myself—from the negative energy of
the outside world.

But then life happens, and my sacred, beautiful home sometimes gets taken over by clutter and chaos. This often happens
when I come home from a work trip. I immediately get busy
with other things and I don't unpack my bag for months. Then I
have to go on another trip, so I dump out what's left in my bag,
leave it in a pile, and pack my bag full of new things. When I
get home, I don't unpack until I have to pack for another trip,
so whatever's left in the bag gets dumped out into another pile.
Right now, I have piles of stuff from four separate trips lying

around, creating stress and chaos in the space that should be my sanctuary.

I admit it—this is really bad. Clutter anywhere in your home represents clutter in your mind. It symbolizes what's going on with you internally. Evolving and growing means dealing with your stuff, whether it's the baggage from your last trip or the baggage in your heart and soul from your childhood. Any stuff that you don't deal with will fester and grow. It must be dealt with for you to move forward. Your home is where you go to rest, to collect yourself, and to feel peaceful and safe. Clutter will always prevent you from feeling this way.

If your home isn't balanced, you'll feel unbalanced inside. Your home is an extension of your physical self, and the physical, emotional, spiritual, and mental parts of you are all connected. I am superaware of how the clutter in my home affects me. When my house is a mess, I can't perform at my best in my professional life. I feel stressed, and this stress bleeds over into my relationships and even my confidence. This is because clutter sucks up energy—something that so many of us are already short on.

The only solution to this is to get rid of the things you don't need. Most of us, even if we don't have a ton of wealth, have way too many things. So many people I know have so much stuff that their houses are full and they have a storage space to keep the overflow. This is crazy to me! Many of them don't even remember what's in there. If they opened up their storage space and looked inside, I bet they'd find a bunch of stuff that they wouldn't want to use again anyway. The few things that they would use again would probably cost much less to buy again new than the fees they're paying every month to store them. Paying for storage every month is literally like paying a fee just to avoid dealing with your life. Is that really worth it?

My own parents are perfect examples of this. Losing everything twice made them even more attached to material things than most people. Possessions took on an emotional meaning to them, and they've become borderline hoarders. My dad has five barbecues. My mom has multiple toasters. She is a master organizer, so you can't see it all, but their house is still full of stuff they don't need or even use.

These things represent their attachment to the past and their fear of losing everything yet again. And I have so much compassion for that. But at the same time, I realize that holding on to things that represent your biggest issues is just another way of grasping tightly to those issues instead of letting go and moving on.

The best times of your life are still ahead of you. If you're holding on to the past mentally and physically by keeping things that remind you of another time, you're not embracing your present life or your bright future. Let go of the past and keep an open heart about your future. Better yet, go out and create a great future for yourself. You can't do this until you let go of the emotions and physical things that are no longer serving you.

I get how hard this is. We're all tired, busy, and overworked, and the last thing any of us want to do is deal with old piles of stuff. But did you ever wonder whether it's those piles of stuff that are making you so tired and anxious? You may think that you've done a good job of squirreling things away under your bed or in a corner of your closet, but that clutter still energetically piles up on your spirit. You need to clear it out and refresh your home with new energy in order to grasp the life you most want.

Home interprets heaven. Home is heaven for beginners.
–CHARLES HENRY PARKHURST

Are you still not convinced that you need the right energy in your home if you want to grow and get more out of life? On *Shahs of Sunset*, Reza was renovating a rental home and was having a ton of problems getting the permits to do the work. I walked through the rooms, trying to pick up on the energy in the space. It wasn't difficult to feel how badly that space needed help. It had bad vibes. When Reza told me about what had happened there (the owners died and their kids had a major fight over their inheritance), it made sense. The space still had those vibes. It needed to be cleaned out.

Have you ever noticed that sometimes when you enter a space you immediately feel a certain way? Sometimes a space feels good and sometimes it feels weird for no apparent reason. Homes have a lot of old energy in them from the people who used to live there. I'm not saying that your house is haunted! But sometimes energy gets stuck. Think about all the people who lived in your home before you and all the people who visited them there over the years. That's probably hundreds of people all together, each with their own unique energy. You need to clean it out and make that space yours.

It's not hard to do this, and it wasn't difficult for me to clear the energy in Reza's property, either. I did exactly what I saw my mother do more than thirty years before. I opened all of the windows and burned a bunch of sage, walking it into every corner of every room. When you burn sage or esphand or one of my favorites, frankincense, it gets into every nook and cranny in the space, even penetrating the wooden beams in the foundation. I did this with intention, bringing positive vibes and love to the space that had been neglected and fought over for so long. It brought newness and freshness and awareness. And the next day, Reza got his permits.

Are you ready to transform your home into your own paradise? No excuses, babe. I don't care how big or small your home is. It can be a mansion or half of a college dorm room. The place you live in should represent not only who you are, but also who you most want to be. It should inspire you. And you have the power to make your space wonderful for you. The rituals in this chapter will help you do it. Like anything in life, it just takes a little bit of energy and intention.

The home should be the treasure chest of living.

—LE CORBUSIER

HOME RITUAL—EVOKE A FEELING

The home rituals in this chapter are a little bit different from the rest of the ones in this book. Instead of doing one main ritual and a few smaller regular rituals, you are going to begin a three-step process to transform your home into your haven. First, you'll clean out the clutter in your home. Then you'll go through your house room by room and add and arrange a few key elements. And finally you'll begin to practice regular daily rituals to honor and enhance your home.

But before you do any of that, it's essential to take a little bit of time to decide what you want the vibe in your home to be like. We so rarely even think about these things, but just as how you can't attract your soul mate until you know what he or she is like, you can't transform your home into your haven until you know what your haven feels like! We all want a "nice" and "comfortable" house, but what does that really mean, lover? How do you want to feel when you step inside of your home after a long day? How do you want guests to feel when they come over?

Sit down with your journal, close your eyes, and imagine your dream home—not the marble kitchen counter and the sweeping ocean views, but the way you'd *feel* in that dream home. You can create the same feeling in your own house, but first you need to know what it is. Do you want to feel peaceful and calm at home or energized and wild? There's no right or wrong answer here. Just be honest with yourself about what you want. Write down three words for how you want to feel in your home.

When you're done, repeat the same exercise for the three key rooms in your home—your bedroom, your kitchen, and your bathroom. How do you want to feel in each of these rooms? For example, for my bedroom my three words are *serene, sensual, sanctuary*. You don't need to use the same ones or use alliteration! Come up with three words for each of these rooms.

Your home is a poem that defines you. When someone comes to your home, what will they know about you? Your home is an extension of who you are. When you come home to a place that makes you feel good, it's like therapy. This takes action. It's up to you to mold and shape the life you want, and that includes your home. Right now, your home is a blank slate. You can create what you want out of it. Take pride in the space you live in and take an active role in creating what you want. The rewards will be priceless.

Now that you know how you want to feel in your home and in each of the key rooms, you can set everything up to evoke that feeling. This is fun and easy! First, though, you have to get rid of everything that *doesn't* evoke that feeling. That means finally dealing with your clutter . . .

Step 1—Clear the Clutter

You are going to do a major clean-out of your home, and it's going to feel amazing. Going through your stuff and deciding which things deserve a role in your life (and which don't) is incredibly healing and empowering. This is a great way to start taking your life to the next level.

Did you see how much my girl MJ's life changed when she

finally agreed to get rid of some of her old stuff on Season 5 of *Shahs of Sunset?* Within weeks, she felt like such a new person that she held a funeral service for her old self and her boyfriend, Tommy, proposed. This is no coincidence, babe. Things will only change when you change something. It's time to make that happen for you.

You can do this all in one day or do it one room at a time over several days. Either way, set aside time for this and psych yourself up. It's going to be fun! If possible, recruit a friend or family member to help you. If not, get pumped to spend some quality time with yourself improving the place you live. Put on some cute, comfy clothes and your favorite music and dance around and have fun while you clean up.

Starting with your closet, go through every room in your house and decide what stays and what goes based on the words you used to describe your dream home. Does the item make you feel that way? No? Then it does not belong in your house. See how simple that is? People always tell me that my home has the best vibe—and they're right. But that's not thanks to some crazy juju magic. I did that to my home by only choosing things that made me feel the way I wanted to feel there. Simple! And you can do the exact same thing. Most people assume that transforming their home means adding a bunch of new stuff, but it's actually more important to take away the things that are detracting from the vibes you want to create in your home.

Closet/Bedroom

You're going to tackle your closet first because pretty much all ladies nowadays suffer from the same cluttered closet chaos.

We have a huge closet (sometimes a whole separate room that we use as a closet) that's overflowing with stuff that we never wear. Meanwhile, we wear the same three or four things every day, and when we have a reason to get dressed up and look cute, we have nothing to wear.

Does this sound familiar? I'm guilty of this, too, lover. I have a huge walk-in closet that's full of clothes, but I wear the same leggings and tank tops almost every day. Then when I have an event to go to, I can't find anything to wear that I feel good in.

Babe, I know, this is so ridiculous! Professional organizers say to hang all of your clothes in your closet with the hangers facing one way and when you wear something, turn it around. After a year, you'll be shocked to see how many things are still not turned around. If you go a whole year without wearing something, you don't need it. You can try this yourself or do a simpler version—go through your closet one item at a time. If you know right away that you want to keep something, then keep it. I'm not trying to force you to get rid of the things you love! But if you're not sure, ask yourself these three questions:

+ Do I need this?

+ When was the last time I wore this?

+ How do I feel in this?

Be honest with yourself! If you don't need it, haven't worn it in a year (or more), and/or don't feel amazing in it, get rid of it. Better yet, find someone who will really love it and give it to her. This is a great way of participating in a generous exchange of energy and adding to the flow of the universe. I promise that goodness will come right back to you in another form.

Before you start making excuses, let me guess—maybe this item is part of a collection or you're going to go get it altered and then you'll love it? No, lover, you won't. I am a big collector of vintage clothes, and I'll tell you the truth—you can't collect everything. If you really do have a collection that is precious to you, fine. Keep a few key things. I have a vintage kaftan collection that I will never get rid of.

But I also have jeans that never fit me—they didn't fit me when I bought them! I tell myself that maybe one day my thighs will fit into them and they'll be magic. But deep down I know they won't. If my thighs ever shrink, I'll have an excuse to buy new jeans. I should give these jeans to someone who can wear and enjoy them today. Likewise, if something is stained, torn, or doesn't fit you, please get rid of it. You must live for the gorgeous body you have today, not the body you'd like to have tomorrow.

After you complete this process, clean all the cobwebs and dust out from the corners of your closet and lovingly put away the clothing that you have decided to keep. This is going to feel so good. And as you move forward, only buy essentials and things you really love. No more buying cheap disposable clothes or things just because they're on sale. So what if it's a good deal? You know what's an even better deal? Spending no money at all. Use and enjoy the things you already have.

When you're done with your closet, move on to the boxes

of things you have squirreled away in the attic and under your bed. A lot of these items may have sentimental value—and I hear that. But you can keep the emotion without keeping the item. In fact, giving these items to someone who can use and enjoy them is a great way to make that emotion last and give these items a new life. For each item, ask yourself whether it makes you feel the way you want in your home. Return to the three words you wrote down. Does this item evoke that feeling?

Paper

I have a major paper problem, and I'm sure you do, too. Where are your piles of bills, mail, and magazines? My problem paper zone is my dining room table. It's like a loading zone for bills, purses, mail, cheese, and everything else I happen to have in my hands when I come home. Since I work from home, it's often also covered with kaftans, invoices, and shipping labels. It is a problem.

You may not have the same situation with the kaftans, but I'll bet you have plenty of paper on your dining, kitchen, or coffee table. It's not going anywhere on its own, so you need to create a system. Find a specific place for unpaid bills, paid bills, and mail. You need a workflow for your bills, or else you'll be tortured by paperwork for the rest of your life. Get rid of any magazines that are more than two months old. If you must keep them for your job, then put them away in a designated place. Everything you keep should have its own place! It sounds so simple, but this rule can completely revolutionize your home for the better.

Kitchen

Even if you spend very little time in your kitchen, take the time to clean it out. Your kitchen is the heart of your home. It represents your health and well-being and is connected to your sensuality. Clutter in your kitchen mirrors the clutter in your heart. Are you spending a lot of time and energy trying to look cute so you can meet your soul mate but leaving your kitchen full of old rotting food and stale snacks? It may sound crazy, but the clutter in your kitchen may be blocking love from flowing directly to you. It's time to clear it out!

Babe, don't lie—I know you have things in your fridge that are so old you don't even remember buying them. Did you actually pack up that salad dressing and move it with you to this house from your last apartment? Face it; some of those hot sauces need to go. And do you even know what's at the bottom of your freezer? What year is that box of Popsicles from? Throw them out right now! This is a way of telling the universe that you care about the place you live. Clean out the pantry. Stop waiting for the apocalypse and give away those old kidney beans that you know you're never going to eat. I doubt you'd crack those things open even if it were the end of the world.

Once you clean it all out, sweep away the old crumbs and only put back foods that nourish your body and spirit.

A house is not a home unless it contains food and fire for the mind as well as the body.

—BENJAMIN FRANKLIN

PRIESTESS POWER POINT:
HOME ON THE ROAD

When I travel, I always make sure to do a few key things to protect myself from the energy of all the people who've stayed in
my hotel room before me and to make myself feel comfortable
and at home wherever I go. I bring a small candle and light it
to create a little sacred space for myself that reminds me of
home. When I enter the room, I open the curtain and all the
windows (if I can) and adjust the temperature. Then I light the
candle to make the scent in the room mine. You'll be surprised
by how much these little things can change the energy in the
room. I also take my shoes off in the hotel room and wear slip-
pers instead. This sends my body and soul a message that when
I am in that room, I am separated from the rest of the world. I
am at home.

Step 2—Add Key Elements

There are simple tweaks you can make to the most important
areas of your home to make your entire home feel like a haven.

Bedroom

This is obviously one of the most important parts of your home.
You spend almost half of your life in this space. You want to feel
good here. The bedroom must be simple and serene. It is a place
that is dedicated to you and your beloved. If you're single, it can

be dedicated to just you. That is special! Don't keep family pictures or heirlooms here. Replace them with items that remind you of special times with your beloved or with yourself.

Try not to have too many electronics in this room. In a perfect world, you wouldn't have any. It's best not to have a TV in your bedroom. Most experts will tell you that the bedroom should only be for sleeping and making love, not watching TV. I'm not perfect. I'll admit that I do have a TV in my bedroom. I love watching movies in bed, but I am disciplined with my TV habits. I don't turn it on all the time—just once in a while when I want to indulge in a late-night movie in bed. If you can't remain disciplined about the TV, keep it out of the bedroom.

You've already created a love altar in your bedroom. Make sure to always keep a plant or fresh flower here. It completely changes the energy of the space, and you'll love waking up to a piece of natural beauty. I also like to burn a candle in my bedroom at night to create a warm, sensual vibe. Find one with a scent you love and enjoy the smell before you drift off to sleep.

Kitchen

A lot of us don't spend much time in the kitchen anymore actually cooking, so this becomes yet another place that is easily cluttered. My parents are the perfect examples of this. On Season 4 of *Shahs*, they moved in with me while I renovated their kitchen to make it perfect for them. They loved it, but within days, their brand-new kitchen was full of clutter. They have three different types of coffeemakers on the counter plus a Keurig that my aunt bought for my mom as a gift (which she never uses, by the way—sorry, Auntie), an electric kettle for tea, and a Persian tea maker.

This is ridiculous! If you have a similar situation in your kitchen, clear off the counter. Only keep things on there that you really use every single day. Everything else should be put in its proper place. If it doesn't have a place, either find one or get rid of it.

There are a few simple things you can add to your kitchen that will bring a lot of life to it. I like to keep a big plate of fresh, colorful vegetables and fruits on my kitchen island. This brings life and nature into my kitchen and it makes me so happy. If you know you're not going to eat all that, just put a few apples and bananas in a bowl on the counter. Give your kitchen some life! Your kitchen isn't just a room to hold your dishes and wine. Food and sensuality go hand in hand, so if you're lacking in the love department, blow some love into your kitchen and see how it manifests in the bedroom.

Bathroom

You probably spend even less time thinking about your bathroom than you do your kitchen, but this is where you get ready to face the day. It's also one of the few places where you spend any time by yourself. The vibe in there is more important than you may realize.

The things you think about in the morning when you're getting ready will set the tone for your entire day. Most of us just naturally think about the things we're worried about or ruminate over the past. But you are the master of your thoughts. If you start living mindfully, your thoughts will change. How do you want to feel in your bathroom? What do you want to think about? Create the space that inspires you with positive thoughts about the future instead of negativity about the past.

I like to hang things in the bathroom that make me feel empowered and inspired. What makes you feel this way? Maybe it's an inspiring quote, a picture that reminds you of a happy time in your life, or a poem. Frame something that's meaningful to you and hang it where you'll see it every morning when you're showering, putting on makeup, and getting ready. These are rituals that you already practice without thinking about them. Adding words that inspire you will make these rituals more intentional and put you in the mind-set you want to be in at the start of your day.

Step 3—Daily Rituals

Now that your home is all set up so that you feel amazing every time you step inside, make sure to keep it that way! These quick daily rituals won't take a lot of time, but they will make a huge difference in the way you feel at home.

Clean the Energy

Every morning I walk through the entire house while burning frankincense. You can also do this with sage or esphand. Smoke energetically clears the space and prepares you for the new day. This is a great way to set your intentions for the day and begin on a positive, proactive note. Remember to walk into every room and corner of your home. It only takes a few moments every day and will make a huge difference.

Deal with Clutter Before It Becomes Clutter

You know as well as I do that once clutter starts, it so easily gets out of control. It snowballs, things get lost, and then suddenly cleaning up the clutter becomes a huge project. You already did that! You don't want to have to do that again. Instead, deal with things as you go. When you get home and you're holding thirty different things, don't just dump them all on the coffee table to deal with later. Deal with them right away by putting them in their place. If any of them don't have a place in your home, maybe you don't need them at all.

Do a Daily Swoop

Even if you deal with things right away, by the end of the day, I bet you'll *still* somehow have a pile of clutter in certain spots in your home. I still have no idea how this happens to me! Every night before bed, do a swoop of your whole house, especially the most common problem areas. Throw away the trash, decide to give away any items that you don't need and aren't using, and put everything else away in its rightful place. Don't just let it sit around and fester.

This will take two minutes if you do it every night, but if you wait for the weekend, it will take all day. Don't let that happen! Do a swoop each evening and wake up every day feeling truly refreshed in your mindfully created and maintained haven on earth.

Home is the nicest word there is.
—LAURA INGALLS WILDER

chapter seven

MAKE FRIENDS WHO ARE LIKE FAMILY

She is a friend of my mind. She gather me, man. The pieces I am, she gather them and give them back to me in all the right order. It's good, you know, when you got a woman who is a friend of your mind.

—TONI MORRISON, *BELOVED*

PRIESTESS PREVIEW

Using the rituals in this chapter, you'll:

✦ Find your tribe of friends who lift you up and raise your energy

✦ Cleanse your current friendships of jealousy and competition

✦ Show mutual appreciation for your closest friends

Maintaining healthy friendships with a carefully chosen golden tribe will make you feel amazing about yourself and your entire life.

Oh, lover, I am so excited to talk to you about friendships! This is one of my favorite topics. Not only are my friendships extremely important to me, but also many of them have been tested on national television. I won't lie—this has not always been easy. But it has given me a ton of strength and taught me a lot about how to nurture and cherish the friendships that really matter and how to compassionately let go of the ones that don't.

As you know, my cousins were my first friends. Those were special relationships because they were my friends and my family. We were young and innocent, and so were our friendships. There was no reason to question them or try to change them. I trusted my cousins and knew they would never stab me in the back. Sure, we still had our share of squabbles and jealousy, but it was normal kid stuff that was really more like sibling rivalry than anything else. I didn't know then how special it was to have these friendships that were based completely on love and trust because I hadn't experienced anything else.

Whether or not they're between family members, childhood friendships are often like this. The things we share with our childhood friends are usually very different from the things that bond us to our adult friends as we get older. As children, we make friends with people based on proximity and time. We have those two things in common. These friends are our siblings or our cousins or our neighbors. They're the girls in our class or the boys on our T-ball team. You live or play near one another and spend time together, and that's what brings you close to one another. There's no reason to question what you have in common or why you became friends in the first place.

Likewise, I never questioned my friendships with my cousins until I was taken away from them. In Germany, I had to actively make friends for the first time in my life, and I had no idea how to do this. It was terrifying! I'm sure it's hard for any new kid at a new school to make friends, but this was next-level hard. The other kids seemed so different from me, and we didn't even speak the same language! I didn't know any of the customs, either. In my culture, we kiss hello on both cheeks. That's what I was used to, and I still do this when I meet someone new. But in Germany it was different. As a greeting, they kiss on one cheek, and being so naive made me feel like even more of an alien than did my Persian nose, black hair, and dark skin!

Even the rules and customs at my new school were completely different in Germany than they were in Iran. My school in Iran was hard-core strict. During the school day, we were either studying or taking tests, period. I'll never forget how I felt when I walked into the German school on that first day and saw the other kids sitting around knitting. Knitting! Suddenly, the bell rang for recess, and everyone ran outside, leaving his or her bags behind in the classroom. I hesitated before following them. In Iran, we always took our bags outside with us. I didn't know what to do, and I didn't speak enough English (or

German) to ask someone whether it was okay to leave my bag behind.

This may seem like such a small thing, but babe, my point is that *everything* was foreign to me. I was completely clueless and alone, and it seemed like it would be impossible to ever connect with the other kids in this strange new place. This time, being in proximity to one another wasn't enough. We still had nothing in common. Or so I thought.

Once I got outside for recess, there was a big part of me that wanted to slink off to the side and just hide. I felt so uncomfortable being out of place and unable to communicate with the other kids. But deep down I knew that hiding would get me nowhere. I had to learn what these kids were all about if I was going to have even the slightest hope of ever fitting in.

Slowly, I walked around the playground and observed the other kids playing. Most of them were doing things I didn't even recognize—playing games I didn't know and speaking to one another in a language I didn't understand. Then I got to a field where a group of kids were playing a game. I watched them split up into two teams and face off as they took turns throwing a ball toward the kids on the other team.

Suddenly, it hit me. Dodgeball! I had played that in Iran. The rules seemed to be a little bit different here, but overall it looked like pretty much the same game. I just watched that day until I understood all the rules, but I went home with a tiny glimmer of hope inside of me. Maybe I would find a way to fit in here.

The next day when the bell rang I left my bag behind like all the other kids and rushed to the field where they'd been playing dodgeball the day before. This time, when they separated into teams, I just sort of slid my way into the group and found myself naturally falling into one of the teams. I had always been athletic as a kid in Iran, and dodgeball had been one of my favorite games. As we started to play, it felt so good to be doing something that I didn't feel insecure about, something I knew I was good at. For the first time since leaving Iran, I felt confident and comfortable. I felt like me.

Who would have thought that dodgeball of all things would end up being my way in with the other kids in Germany? But it was. For the next few years, I remained friends with those kids I met on the playground and the ones I hung out with later when I started taking a gymnastics class, but as I grew and evolved, so did my friendships.

I came into my own in Germany. It was during my years there that I became the woman I am today. There, I was exposed to so many exciting new things—politics, culture, and intellectualism. I grew up, and I gained a set of convictions. I got into art and literature and feminism—pretty heavy stuff for a preteen! But I had already been through so much in my life, and I felt like a warrior. It became difficult for me to feel like I had anything in common with the kids at school who had been born and raised in one place and remained quite sheltered. I had nothing against those kids—they were fun to play with—but we didn't have the history that I shared with my cousins or enough shared interests or experiences to keep us close.

At around that time, I started becoming friends with other refugee kids who had come to Germany from all over the world—Yugoslavia, Russia, and Africa. Our backgrounds and cultures were completely different, but we shared similar experiences. Each of us had left our families and countries behind and started over in Germany. That was huge. We also soon learned that we shared a love of hip-hop.

When I started hanging out with these hip-hop kids, my parents got nervous. I had always been a good student, and I still was. My new friends . . . not so much. They were always getting into trouble in school, and my parents hated the fact that I was hanging out with the "bad" kids from "bad families." We were street kids.

I was a good kid. That didn't change, but I still had more in common with those kids who were from the fringes of society than I did with the ones who were still so innocent and naive. My eyes had been opened, and I couldn't shut them again now. I could be myself around those other refugee kids. They didn't judge me or look down on me, and being around that energy gave me the freedom to find myself.

By the time I moved to Los Angeles, it was a whole new ball game. Once again, my family had to leave everything behind. We packed one bag each, making hard decisions about what to bring with us, and moved to a new country. This time, to a place where everyone seemed to have everything they'd ever wanted. They weren't sheltered; they were privileged.

But it was different for me this time because now I knew who I was. It didn't matter that I didn't have the same clothes as the other girls. I was comfortable in my clothes and in my own skin, and my style reflected my true self—my golden Inner

Priestess. It was a flag that I used to attract the other artists and "vierdos," who quickly became my friends.

The funny thing about moving to Beverly Hills was that this time, everyone there looked like me! This was the first time I had been around other Persian people since leaving Iran seven years earlier. About sixty-five percent of the kids at Beverly were Persian. I was so excited to finally fit in, and I assumed I'd have plenty of things in common with these other Persian kids. I soon found out that wasn't the case. They may have been Persian, but their lives were totally and completely different from mine. They had grown up in Beverly Hills, not Iran. Most of their families had left Iran before the revolution, so they'd been able to bring their wealth with them.

We didn't even share the same customs. Instead of kissing on both cheeks, they either kissed on one cheek or hugged each other. (After living in so many places, I have a whole repertoire of greetings in my head, which often leads to greeting confusion, but I still prefer the two kisses of my culture.)

It didn't take long for me to discover that I had much more in common with the group of creative kids who were culturally and ethnically diverse. While Beverly Hills High School wasn't particularly diverse, my group of friends was. Our similarities ran deeper than our religions, cultures, or the colors of our skin.

We all use certain codes to tell the world who we are. These codes attract certain people to us; they make a statement. For me at the age of seven in Germany, that code was something as simple as a game of dodgeball. I was able to tell the other kids that I was one of them by playing with them. At Beverly, my code was my style. As soon as I got there, I could spot my tribe just by looking at them. They were the ones wearing hip-hop-style clothing—street style. I knew right away that those were my peeps.

As I've continued to evolve since then, these codes have evolved, too. They have become the deeper core values that my friends and I share—love, respect, and trust. If you have those things in common, who cares about anything else?

There is a magnet in your heart that will attract true friends. That magnet is unselfishness, thinking of others first; when you learn to live for others, they will live for you.
—PARAMAHANSA YOGANANDA

As an adult, my friendships are now based on these three core values and one secret ingredient—the fact that we simply like one another. It's an amazing surprise for someone to come into your life by destiny or chance and become as close as family. That's how I feel about my closest friends. I have a lot of acquaintances, but my closest inner circle is small and they are sacred to me. They are my golden tribe. I trust these people with my life and completely depend on them.

These friendships are incredibly special. We weren't assigned to one another at school or at birth. We didn't settle for one another. Instead, we recognized something in one another that resonated within us and made us want to spend time together. That's amazing!

Unlike family relationships that come with a lot of baggage or relationships with a partner that always carry the weight of a lot of expectations, friendships are completely free of these burdens. They can be whatever you want them to be. I'm in awe of the fact that I can be as close to some of my friends as I am with my family and care about them so much even though we're not biologically connected. My adult friendships have been some of the greatest surprises in my life.

I know how rare it is to find people who truly care about me and have my back in this crazy competitive world. My life has been blasting at full volume since I was a child. Nothing about it is chill. And when I find people in this world who have a beautiful heart and are strong enough to roll with me through this craziness, I hang on to them for dear life and give our friendships everything I've got.

Just like every other part of your life, your friendships should be active and intentional. It's not enough to just let a friendship happen. That's not how amazing things are created! No, it shouldn't be hard work, but your friendships should be purposeful. They should have meaning. What do you want to get out of your friendships? How do you want to make your friends feel? What sort of people do you want to allow into your inner golden circle?

If you've already completed the Priestess Detox, you've probably discovered that you have a few negative friends in your life. It's important to protect yourself from these people— not just to avoid their negativity but also because staying away from them frees you up to find other, more positive friends.

Our friendships are important vehicles for change. Your friends can help you grow and evolve more than anyone else in your life. But only if you choose your friends wisely and become an active friend yourself. Start taking your role as a friend seriously. It's an important one—one of the most important roles you'll ever play.

I give a lot to my friends and I expect a lot from them in return. I'm not talking about giving them material things (though I do love giving gifts to my friends, too). I mean giving my time, my energy, my love, and my heart. In return, I expect my friends to treat me with love, honesty, and respect. That doesn't mean I'm always falsely positive and sit around telling my friends how great they are. I give honest, loving feedback (along with plenty of compliments straight from the heart). Likewise, I don't want friends who only tell me what they think I want to hear! I know that in order to grow, I need loving friends who aren't afraid to be honest. That means I have to be open to receiving constructive feedback as well as praise.

My relationship with Mike from *Shahs of Sunset* is the perfect example of this. I've known Mike since I moved to Beverly Hills when I was fifteen. After moving to two new continents as a child, I don't have any childhood friends anymore. This is the longest that any of my friends have been in my life. If you watched Season 5 of *Shahs*, you already know that Mike went through an incredibly hard time during that season. He messed up in his marriage, and he admitted this to all of us and owned up to his mistakes.

A lot of people judged Mike for what he did—and I'm not excusing it—but I knew that my job as his friend wasn't to stomp on him when he was already down and point fingers at him. He already knew what he had done wrong. Making him feel worse would not help him grow or allow him to take back what he did. Instead, I gave him space and simply let him know that I was there for him when he needed me.

Mike and I are very different people, but we actually grew a lot closer when he was going through this hardship and I was there for him. It bonded us together. He also found a new spiritual side of himself during this time that I was able to connect with. This brought us closer than ever, and I'm so grateful for that.

MJ is another friend whom I expect a lot from. Well, not a lot. I expect the same three things from her that I expect from everyone: love, respect, and trust. I believe friends should accept each other for who they are—flaws and all—while helping each other reach our highest potential. I always tried to see the best in MJ, but after consistently giving our friendship my all in the face of continuous gossip, I had to protect myself by taking my distance.

If you saw the Season 5 reunion of *Shahs of Sunset*, you know that my friendship with MJ has grown completely dysfunctional. Unfortunately, it's been this way for a long time. It's unbalanced, and endless backstabbing has eroded the trust between us. Without that trust, there is no friendship. We can still hang out and have fun together, but when there's no trust, the deeper friendship is over.

In the cutthroat world I live in, there's a ton of gossip and fake people who I know smile at me and then talk about me behind my back. I have to protect myself from that, especially because I have such an open heart. It's okay to have different types of friendships that serve different purposes in your life. Not everyone you like or have fun with is going to end up in your golden tribe.

Growing up, I had a friend named Kathy whom I went dancing with at all the underground clubs. She was my dance buddy, and we always had a blast together. We didn't have deep conversations about life and spirituality, and I didn't expect to. I save that for my golden tribe. I need them, and I expect them to need me, too. We take turns supporting and challenging and loving one another.

This has to be balanced. You can't give a hundred percent to your friends and accept ten percent in return or vice versa. Instead, you have to give your friends at least as much as you expect from them in return. That's the minimum. Of course, it's not about keeping track of who has done what for whom. Don't ever keep score. But if you're constantly giving or constantly taking, that's not a true friendship. And that's not cool.

My friendship with GG was like this for a while. For years she was verbally abusive, she called me names, and she even got physical with me at one point. A lot of people wondered why I even kept her in my life at all, but it was clear to me that she was lashing out at me based on problems that actually had nothing to do with me. I always had compassion for her because I knew that inside she was hurting. But when things got physical, I had to take a step back, draw a line, and protect myself.

I set boundaries, but I never cut GG out of my life completely. We actually spent a lot of time together off camera during this time. I made it clear that I wouldn't tolerate being treated badly but that I was there for her if she was willing to treat me with love, respect, and trust. Eventually, she responded and really opened up to me. Now I'm so glad that I stuck around through those hard times, because we found a beautiful place in our friendship. I want nothing but the best for her, and I believe she feels the same way about me.

After doing the Priestess Detox, you know which friends you need to protect yourself from. Do you need to cut them out of your life or simply draw boundaries? It's up to you, lover, but you must do what is best for you. Remember, if someone is negative or toxic, that doesn't make him or her a bad person. He or she is just at a point in their journey where they can't be there for their friends.

When GG attacked Adam in Season 5 of *Shahs of Sunset*, Reza was done with her. He felt that he had tried everything to get their friendship to a more positive place and he couldn't continue to have so much negativity in his life. I understood this. If you put effort into a friendship and it's continuously abusive, you don't have to keep taking it. You have the power to decide how much you're willing to take. Examine whether or not you want to continue down a path with this person. No matter what this person has meant to you in the past, you do have a choice.

Perhaps the greatest surprise in my life over the last few years has been growing so much closer to Reza. Our friendship is unique. It's not like the ones I shared with my childhood friends. Reza and I have known each other for a while, but we weren't always so close. We don't share a past. Instead, we share the joy of the moment together. We've also been through a lot of deep experiences together. When we went together to the border of Iran—the closest either of us has been to our home-land since we were young children—we bonded in a whole new way. Reza and I don't agree on everything. We have seri-ous political disagreements, and we're very different people. But we have a soul connection and mutual love, respect, and trust. That's all that matters.

When you meet someone whom you just click with and enjoy being with, it's such a joy. It's magic. And it's really not that different from meeting your soul mate. When I'm feeling down, just spending an hour with Reza cracking up together changes my whole vibe. We don't even need to talk about my problems. Just being together is healing and shifts me into a place of joy. That is something money can't buy.

Your friend is your needs answered.

–KAHLIL GIBRAN

⟨⟩ STEP 1—FIND YOUR GOLDEN TRIBE ⟨⟩

Lover, I know you may be thinking, *Okay, this is all great, but I don't have those kinds of friends in my life!* That's okay. It's never too late to find your golden tribe. Attracting the right friends into your life is a lot like attracting your soul mate. You will attract people who are on your wavelength, who are living similar lives with a similar energy as you. Don't like the friends you currently have in your life? It's time to find out why by looking in the mirror.

The more you get out there and work on getting yourself to an amazing golden place in your life, the closer you'll get to your Inner Priestess. And it's on this path that you'll be able to manifest your tribe or attract more people to add to your tribe.

Not only will you attract people with a similar vibration, you'll also naturally start to mirror your friends' energy once they're in your inner circle. This is why it's so important to choose friends who are confident, strong, and loving. You're flying together on the same path. If you're trying to fly higher, you don't want people weighing you down.

I know it can be hard to meet people in this crazy world. Except for school and work, we mostly connect to one another through technology. Sometimes we rarely see or even speak to the people we consider close friends. This has turned us into little islands that only connect to one another through our phones.

If you don't have a golden tribe that you're excited about, it's up to you to change something. Staying at home and looking at

Instagram isn't going to help. Get out there and do the things that make you feel alive, the things that make you feel like you. Remember, it's on this path that you'll attract the people who have the same energy as you.

What do you love to do more than anything? Is it yoga, writing, knitting, or experimenting with funky makeup? Write down the top three things that you're passionate about. It can be anything you find fun and exciting, not necessarily something that's connected to your job or education. These can be hobbies or secret passions that you find intriguing. Then next to each thing, write down a place where you can go to find like-minded people. This can be a class, a conference, or anywhere you'll find a crowd of people whom you already have something in common with. Some great examples are a yoga class, a screenwriting class, or a concert. These are the perfect places to meet friends because the people there already share something meaningful with you. You're passionate about the same things. Go to these places and be open to the people around you.

This may sound scary or intimidating, lover, but what do you have to lose? It may take some time and some trial and error to get this right. Maybe you'll go to a meditation meet-up and completely hate it. That's okay! Try something else next time. Keep returning to the list of things you're passionate about. They will eventually steer you toward the people who share your values.

It's up to you to actively drive your life. Even if you feel closed off and scared, go anyway. Energetically, the more active you are, the more open you'll be. When you pursue your passions, you fall into the synchronicity of the universe. The universe wants to help you find your golden tribe—you just have to put yourself out there!

Getting out of your routine and becoming a part of a community is how you'll evolve. Adult friendships should feel incredible, with no baggage or drama. If yours don't feel that way, it's time to make a change. You can only do that by changing something. Remember, the people you surround yourself with will in many ways define who you are. Your friends aren't people whom you just kill time with, like someone you're standing next to while waiting for the bus. No, lover! Friendship is the most beautiful vehicle for growth. If you're not getting this from your friends, honestly ask yourself whether you're in the right tribe. I promise yours is out there waiting for you to fly higher with them!

In the sweetness of friendship let there be laughter, and sharing of pleasures. For in the dew of little things the heart finds its morning and is refreshed.

–KAHLIL GIBRAN

STEP 2—CLEANSE YOUR FRIENDSHIPS OF JEALOUSY AND COMPETITION

Too often, we end up repeating toxic patterns from our family relationships in our friendships. This is how strong the baggage from our parents is! You must rid yourself of this baggage by

completing the family rituals before moving on to improving your friendships. If you've already done the family rituals, you have so much more awareness about some of the toxic patterns that may be popping up in your friendships. Take some time to think about this. You can change this dynamic, but you have to be honest with yourself about what role you're playing and be willing to make a change.

Unfortunately, the toxic patterns in most friendships hav to do with jealousy and competition. I'm going to say this onc and I really want you to hear me. True friends cannot be jea ous of each other. Okay, fine, I'll say it again. True friends ca not be jealous of each other. That's because true friends wa their friends to succeed. They want their friends to rise up. Th know that we all rise when we lift each other up. Your frier success does not take anything away from you. If anythin lifts you higher because your life will naturally reflect wl going on with your friends. Your friend's happiness is a v derful thing.

Be honest with yourself, lover. When something good pens to one of your friends, do you feel a pang of jealous when something bad happens to one of them, do you fe a little bit happy about it? It's okay if the answer is yes. all human, and we all have some amount of envy in us. normal. But it's important to pay attention to *why* you fe way so you can change the dynamic.

When you're feeling jealous of someone else, you're ing on that person and his or her life instead of on your your life. This is a big deal because that energy that you

ing by feeling jealous is stopping you from getting what you want in your life! In fact, most of the time when someone is jealous of someone else, it's because they feel negative or guilty about the lack of positive action in their own life. They see their friend doing awesome things and finding success, and it just reminds them of all the things they're not doing in their own life. Instead of using these feelings as fuel to get motivated, they get it twisted and lash out at the person who they believe caused that bad feeling.

But lover, if this is you, you need to know that your friend's success did not cause that negative feeling. Your friend actually has nothing to do with that feeling. You caused that feeling by not taking action and failing to go after what you want in this world. I really do not mean to sound harsh, but this is so important! Look at it this way—it's a good thing you caused this bad feeling because that means you are the one who has the power to turn it around. If you created it, you can take it away. And you can do this by getting into action instead of wasting time and energy being jealous of your friends. Jealousy is the thief of happiness and success. Don't let it steal those things from you!

This is something I've unfortunately dealt with in a lot of my friendships. I've sometimes had trouble sharing my joy and accomplishments with friends because they're not happy for me. Why not? Well, they're not really out there pursuing their dreams, so they're jealous of my success. But look, we all have the same twenty-four hours in a day. You, me, Beyoncé, everyone. I work all day, every day. That's how I've become successful.

It's up to you to decide what you'll do with your precious hours. Are you going to use them to get what's yours or sit around being jealous of the people who do?

Reza and I have made it a point to be proud of each other for all of our accomplishments. I know that he's going to get his and I'm going to get mine. One doesn't detract from the other. When you work hard for something like Reza and I both have, you see the value in it and you wouldn't want to take that away from anyone.

Whenever you start feeling jealous or competitive with a friend, stop and check yourself. Get that monkey to stop rattling his cage for just a minute and pull your mind from racing in that direction. That wheel of jealousy can turn very fast, and sometimes one Instagram picture is all it takes to send you down a negative spiral. A lot of this does start with social media, where most people portray themselves as perfect and happy and successful. That has little to do with the truth. You know that. Everyone on there is marketing themselves and their lives, and you're falling for it. When you feel this happening, take a break. Put your phone down. Just stop.

Now ask yourself two questions: What am I grateful for, and what am I doing to grow and evolve? Take a moment to remember all of the things you were given by the universe. Not everyone is given everything but everyone is given something. What were you given? We all have assets. You need to find yours to start cultivating your golden Inner Priestess.

Certain qualities are valued more by our society than others, so you may not even be aware of all your beautiful qualities. Are you great with animals? Are children drawn to you? Do you have a head for numbers and finances? Or do people naturally feel comfortable talking to you? Be grateful for these things! They are gifts, and not everybody has them.

But it's not enough to simply be aware of your gifts. You have to use them. Talent plus dedication and work ethic—that's how you get success. This is why you must ask yourself what you're doing to fly in the direction of your dreams. Are you working on your art, getting an advanced degree, learning from a mentor, or kicking ass at your job?

If you're not doing these things, you don't have to be jealous of the people who are—just start doing them. Jealousy is a distraction. It's a false way of focusing on the other person. It's really not about him or her. It's about the fact that you feel bad for not doing the things you know you should. Well, how do you solve that? Start doing them, lover. Stop looking at what other people are doing and focus on you. Whatever you put your energy and talents toward will grow. Focus every bit of your beautiful golden energy on yourself. Make yourself grow. That is how you'll cleanse your friendships, your soul, and your precious golden life.

Friendship is unnecessary, like philosophy, like art . . . It has no survival value; rather it is one of those things that give value to survival.

–C. S. LEWIS, *THE FOUR LOVES*

PRIESTESS POWER POINT: TAKE FIVE

On reality TV, it feels like I am always surrounded by people's reactions. When you react to something right away, you don't give yourself a chance to make a good decision. You are letting your emotions control you. On the show, I always felt that my power came from intentionally choosing my path instead of immediately reacting to whatever was going on around me. This sounds hard, but it's actually really easy. When something happens and you want to react, just stop whatever you're doing and wait five seconds. That's it! Count to five in your head as you consciously decide how to react. This will give you so much more power over the way you act and react to everything in your life.

⊸ STEP 3—CHERISH ⊸ YOUR FRIENDSHIPS

Once you have found your golden tribe and cleansed it of any jealousy or competition that may have been lurking in those relationships, it's time to nurture and cherish your precious, sacred friendships. In case you haven't noticed by now, a lot of the rituals in this book are about cherishing the positive things in your life. That's how you get more of them! Friendships are definitely one of these things. They are so special and bring more peace and happiness than most people realize.

If you're not getting enough from your friendships, the best thing you can do is give more. Actively cultivate this relationship. Like so many other things in life, this all comes down to making an effort. This doesn't have to be complicated or expensive. Here are some easy ways to cultivate your friendships:

✦ Get into an active mode together

Take a class together or start running together. Move together toward mutual growth. Your friendships are great vehicles for change and growth. Use them!

✦ Be sensitive and unselfish

When you talk on the phone to your friends, make sure you're not only talking about your problems. Strive for balance. Be sensitive to your friend's needs. A lot of people don't ask for help when they need it, but if you pay attention, you'll notice when a friend seems down or out of sorts. Ask him or her about it. Actively listen and try to help find solutions. This isn't about being nosy or irritating. Instead, be sensitive to what your friend is going through. Maybe just talking about it is really hard for him or her. Let him or her know that with you, there's a safe environment to talk about anything. Work to create that non-judgmental, loving, and honest environment where your friends can be themselves.

✦ Be in the moment

I've noticed lately that whenever I'm with friends in a beautiful setting, they want to take pictures to post online. I understand this impulse, and I do it sometimes, too. But when we do this, we're just documenting the moment instead of being in the moment. The next time you're with your friends, put your phone down and just be. Focus on them. Pay attention. You'll connect with your friends on a deeper level if you're not distracting yourself by trying to create a certain image on social media.

✦ Make an effort

Back in high school I used to make mix tapes and collages to go with them for my friends. They were unique, one-of-a-kind creations, and they were so special. People don't do things like this as much anymore. It's easier to just go to the mall and buy a gift. But putting thought and time into something is always worth so much more.

✦ Create your own ritual

Just like you're creating a family ritual to share a meal with one another, find a small but meaningful ritual to share with your golden tribe. This will nurture the friendships for years to come. Between seasons of *Shahs of Sunset*, there's a period of time when we're not shooting, and we love to hang out together. Last year, Reza had an idea to go to this health spa in Mexico. It was the kind of place that had sports classes, healthy food, yoga, meditation, swimming—you name it. MJ, Reza, and I went together, and we affectionately referred to it as "fat camp" because we all wanted to get in shape while we were there. We all stayed together in our little cabin, and the first morning we got up at five thirty to go for a hike. We were miserable and grumpy at first, but Reza got up and blasted Rihanna to get us up and moving. Day by day, that became our ritual—listening to Rihanna as we woke up and got ready for the day.

To this day, whenever I hear Rihanna, I think of those happy times with my friends. Rituals can be as simple as listening to a song, sharing a meal, or going on a lavish vacation. Make the memories you want to share, and cherish them.

Friendship is always a sweet responsibility, never an opportunity.

–KAHLIL GIBRAN

FRIENDSHIP RITUAL— CREATE A MUTUAL APPRECIATION SOCIETY

You'll need: a friend!

Time allotted: 1 hour

Of course, you're going to do this ritual with a friend. Pick a member of your golden tribe or do this one by one with every member of your tribe. Plan a time to go somewhere together where you're both comfortable and happy. It can be a coffee shop, a park, a restaurant, or wherever you both feel good. Sit down together and get comfortable, and when the time is right turn to your friend.

Look him or her in the eyes and say, "Let's play a game. I want to do a ritual with you. I'll start and then let's go back and forth and tell each other what we appreciate about each other." It's important that you go first to make your friend feel comfortable (and because you've had more time to prepare!). Your friend might resist at first. That's okay. Maybe he or she thinks it sounds cheesy or goofy. Don't push—just go ahead with your turn any-way. Hearing what you have to say will open the other person up and put him or her in the right frame of mind to take a turn.

When you're thinking about what to say, dig deep, and be really honest. You can say anything as long as it's positive and true. Maybe it's "I love that you always make me laugh" or "I feel great knowing that I can completely trust you" or even "I love the fact that you call me on my drama and make me be a better person." It will feel good to say this out loud to your friend! If he or she can't think of anything to say back, that's okay. Don't push it. I bet in time, they'll come around and think of lots of wonderful things to say about you.

Doing this really develops the generosity between you and your friends. Anytime you can develop those skills, you're grow-ing exponentially. You're practicing the opposite of jealousy, and that is so powerful.

Don't just do this once and then forget it. Do this ritualisti-cally with your friends.

We actually do this once every season on *Shahs of Sunset.* There's always some drama or fighting going on, so I pull every-one into a circle and say, "Let's go around and take turns saying what we love about one another."

Despite how great this is, I always prefer to do this ritual one-on-one. I recently went to lunch with Reza for his birthday and I surprised him with this ritual. I said to him:

I love that when I'm in a bad mood or stressed I can see you and hang and it totally and completely changes my vibe.

I love that you crack me up so much.

I'm so grateful for your loyalty as a friend.

I can totally one million percent rely on you no matter what.

You have equally great taste and are fun to go shopping with!

Reza responded with the following:

You're very loving and take good care of your friends and family.

You're a go-getter, aggressive, and you do everything expeditiously.

You have a special unique sense of style and you express it with pride and confidence.

You have a passion for food and we can bond on what's really important in life, RAMEN!!!!

You're smart!

Rare as is true love, true friendship is rarer.

—JEAN DE LA FONTAINE

chapter eight

STYLIN' AND PROFILIN' FOR LIFE

Everything that is made beautiful and fair and lovely is made for the eye
of one who sees.

—RUMI

PRIESTESS PREVIEW

Through the rituals in this chapter, you'll learn to:

✦ Develop your own personal style

✦ Push the boundaries of your style

✦ Keep evolving your style as you grow and change

It feels amazing to dress in a way that expresses your inner soul.
I can't wait for you to experience this!

First things first, lover. What is style? Some people think it's as simple as the clothes you wear, as long as they look nice. But no. That's fashion, and I think there's actually a huge difference between fashion and style.

Style is not something you can buy with money. It's a little bit of magic and a whole lot of you. It's the visual representation of your Inner Priestess—the way you share your beautiful, golden essence with the world. Can you tell that I think style is a little bit important? Well, I'll tell you why style is so important to me.

You already know that when I was a child I had to keep leaving behind everything familiar in my life. There were only a few things I could hold on to—my family, of course, and the rituals that helped me feel grounded. The other thing I was able to grasp on to as I repeatedly lost the ground under my feet was my sense of style.

Think about it this way—when you have to pack up one small suitcase and leave your home in a sudden rush for whatever reason, there are a few things you'd definitely take with you. Clothing is one of them. So the clothing and other items that I brought with me from continent to continent took on a special meaning. They became precious to me. While I had my culture, my rituals, and my family to ground me, my clothes were the only physical things I held on to that connected me to my childhood, my culture, and my homeland.

As I got older, I began to find ways to use these items as a visual representation of myself and combined elements of everything I'd been exposed to in order to create my unique, signature style. At the time, I wasn't fully aware of what I was doing. I didn't have enough money to afford the nice, fashionable clothes that the other kids at school wore, so I simply took the items I had access to and used them to create my own thing.

Looking back now, I can see that my childhood was so disjointed. The things I saw before the war, during the war, after moving to Germany, and then after moving to Los Angeles varied so wildly. In a way, combining the visual elements of each of these fragmented pieces was my way of patching together the scraps of my life, little by little making it whole.

My earliest visual memories are of my grandmother in Iran wearing beautiful, flowing kaftans. She had a traditional nose piercing and tribal tattoos in her younger days and was breathtakingly stunning. It wasn't only her physical beauty that made her so striking; it was also her confidence and the pride she clearly took in the way she presented herself to the world. There was so much ancient poetry in her look, and that made a huge impression on me. She was my first image of true, womanly beauty.

My grandmother's style was a complete contrast to the way my mother and aunties presented themselves. They were modern, sexy, and fly in their 1970s miniskirts and platform boots. Yes, they were stunning, too, but in a completely different way.

They were a bright, shining representation of the new world and the future, while my grandmother was a romantic image of the ancient past.

Of course, the styles I saw in Iran changed with the revolution. Suddenly, all of the women and girls—my grandmother, my mother, my aunties, and even me—were forced to wear a veil anytime we were in public. This made the people around me look completely different, and as a child I was struck by the fact that something as simple as a veil could totally change the way someone presented themselves to the world. To me, the women were just as beautiful and glamorous with the veil on, but now they were starker and more mysterious. This was a lesson in aesthetics and the way relatively small things can change your whole vibe.

It was also shocking to suddenly have restrictions placed on us about what we could and couldn't wear. This was completely new to me, and it made a huge impression. At that time in my life, I completely lost the option to use my style as a form of self-expression. I had to dress and look a certain way. It wasn't only looked down upon to dress differently, it was illegal. Of course one of the main reasons my parents decided to flee from Iran and move to Germany was to gain more freedom. One of the many freedoms we longed for was to dress however we wanted. I never took that for granted.

So before I even moved away from my homeland, I had experienced a vast universe of style. I had also seen how beauty could stem from such extremes—from tribal and contemporary Western to traditional garb—and realized that style, glamour, and beauty were completely versatile. Style was everywhere, and it wasn't just one thing. In fact, I saw that it could be created in an endless multitude of ways.

Then I went from the veiled world of the Iranian revolution to 1980s Germany, where the punk movement was just starting to take hold. As I walked through the streets of Hamburg, my eyes boggled at the explosion of street style that was going on around me. The city streets were bursting with early hip-hop style: ripped denim and bomber jackets, studded leather, Mohawks, wild prints, and lots of gold chains.

Right away, I noticed how unique and individualistic the people in Germany were. They weren't fashionable; they were stylish. These people were not mindlessly buying the same boring clothes as everyone else or even just choosing their clothes for comfort. They were using their clothes as a form of self-expression. People of every age—from young teenagers to senior citizens—were rocking crazy, unique styles. I soaked it all up, inspired. But I had no desire to just copy these looks entirely. That wouldn't be me. Instead, I had a strong urge to patch elements of this look together with the foundation of style I'd formed in Iran.

This was when I started piecing together the different elements of everything I'd been exposed to and began to create my own unique style. I was still a young preteen. Even in Germany, most of the kids my age didn't really care about style. But I felt a need to process everything I'd been through. So I began experimenting.

After seeing so many different forms of "normal" at a young

age, I didn't ascribe to any traditional sense of what "normal" was anymore. And I certainly didn't care what anybody else thought or said about what I wore. There were no rules to my style, no norms I was willing to follow. All that mattered to me was that the things I wore represented a piece of me and my unique history. Other than that, it was a fashion free-for-all.

My style was wild. I'd wear a traditional veil from Iran with a miniskirt and Jordans or an acid-washed denim minidress with knee-high socks, huge sneakers, sunglasses, and tribal jewelry. At the time, combining elements of Eastern and Western culture was totally new. People thought it was crazy. But no one could tell me that it was wrong.

In one of my favorite pictures of myself from this time, I'm wearing a classic young Asa outfit—black tights and a turquoise T-shirt underneath my mom's flowing green skirt that I wore around my shoulders as a cape and a Persian tablecloth that I fastened around my waist to look like a wrap skirt. Around my neck are crystal necklaces. Giant gold earrings dangle from my ears, and of course I have some fly Jordans on my feet. The best part of the picture, though, is the look on my face. I am in ecstasy, drunk with the freedom to be no one else but me.

I didn't wear any of this for shock value or attention. Not at all, lover! It was just my way of expressing myself. I wanted people to look at me and know something about me beyond simply what store I shopped in. My style became my visual history, a badge of honor for everything I'd been through. Getting dressed in the morning was now my favorite activity. It was an art form, a mode of self-expression. Every morning when I decided what to wear, I felt a sense of solace and peace come over me. No matter how crazy the world around me may have been, my style was the one thing I had that was just mine. It was the one time I had complete freedom to do whatever I wanted, and I knew the true value of that freedom.

Of course, everyone had a different reaction to my style. I got tons of feedback, both bad and good. Most of the time people just said, "Asa's style is so crazy." Thankfully, my parents never tried to stop me from dressing the way I wanted. They just let me be myself. I'm sure they were completely confused by some of my outfits! But they could also see how good I felt in whatever I was wearing, and they weren't going to try to put a damper on that. I was so happy to have the freedom to be radically myself. Isn't it crazy that it's such a drastic and even controversial idea in our society to be radically yourself? We all try to shoehorn ourselves into these rigid boxes that limit us and force us to play small. There's no room in those boxes for individuality. True beauty only comes from being radically you.

It was around this time that I also started buying vintage clothing. Babe, this was in the late eighties, *way* before buying vintage was a cool thing to do. Vintage clothing barely existed back then. It wasn't even a thing yet. While all of my friends thought the idea of buying "used" clothes was strange, I loved the idea that these items of clothing had a history and that each one was a one-off.

It was fun to imagine how their original owners put them together with other items to create their own unique looks, but to me the best part was that each item in the store was unique. Unlike in chain stores with mass-produced items, in the vintage stores there was only one of each thing. Whoever wore it would be an original. More practically, it was also an easy way to get high-quality clothing for less money.

The first time I went into a vintage shop in Hamburg, I bought an amazing pair of burgundy velvet pants and a fly seventies leather jacket that I never would have been able to afford to buy new. That was the day that my love for vintage clothes was born. Over the next few years, I became a curator, adding pieces that spoke to my unique sensibilities and represented a part of me.

My vintage collection became so precious to me that when my family moved to Los Angeles a few years later, I brought several pieces with me. I still have many of them! They took up most of the room in my one allotted suitcase, forcing me to leave behind some of my most prized photos, books, and other belongings. But I couldn't give them up. My vintage items were unique and—like the photos—could never be replaced. They were my treasures.

These are some of my very favorite vintage pieces that have traveled with me from Germany to Beverly Hills and beyond:

✦ My early 1980s super-sequined Caché bolero jacket (I love a great bolero)

✦ A 1970s long super-colorful paisley velvet coat with gold embroidery detail with a deep purple lining (this coat is out of this world)

✦ Perhaps the most epic kaftan collection in the world from all around the globe

✦ A major and very large collection of seventies, eighties, and nineties leather jackets, including a 1980s purple motorcycle jacket

✦ A huge collection of 1970s maxi dresses (this is all I wore from 1998 to 2003)

✦ All my nineties outfits that I don't really consider vintage because I am a nineties baby for life!

Fashion fades, only style remains the same.

−COCO CHANEL

By the time I arrived in America, my sense of style was completely developed. My boy Mike from *Shahs of Sunset* still remembers (and teases me about) the outfit I wore on my first day at Beverly Hills High School—some fresh Jordans, a mini-skirt, a high ponytail, and a dope yellow denim jacket. That jacket was my absolute fave. One good thing about my mom being such a hoarder is that she never got rid of it! I recently rescued it from her attic and brought it back home with me. It took a few washes to get the smell of mothballs out, but it was worth it!

Before leaving Germany, I imagined that the people in Beverly Hills would look so fresh and all have crazy style, and the reality turned out to be very different from what I expected. At Beverly, I didn't see the unique forms of self-expression that I was bombarded with in Germany. I was so excited to be around other Persian kids again, but I was immediately put in a different category than the other Persian girls because of my style.

In Beverly Hills, there was so much pressure to conform, and nobody there seemed to understand my style. The other girls all shopped at the same stores and wore the same things. They technically looked good—they had money to buy expensive clothes and shoes, and their outfits were well put together—but to me, they just looked boring. I didn't understand the point of spending all that money on clothes just to look like everyone else.

The difference in style between me and the other Persian girls could not have been more striking. They went shopping and bought whatever happened to be in at the time. My style was all about searching for specific things that represented who I was and then putting them together to make them completely my own. But I felt that I had less freedom to express myself in Beverly Hills than I did in Germany. The other Persian girls were extremely preppy. Next to them, I looked like a rebel in my wild outfits.

I understood that the differences between those other girls and me went deeper than our clothes. They'd never been given the kind of freedom to express themselves that I experienced in Germany, but they'd never suffered the complete lack of it, either. Their families had all left Iran before the war. They didn't know what it was like to be forced to dress and look a certain way, so their self-expression wasn't as important to them. They were happy all dressing the same, and I didn't judge them for it, but my agenda was to do whatever it took to be an individual. It was my therapy, and at the time, it was also my art. It took me a long time to gain the courage to call myself an artist, so for years I poured every ounce of my creative energy into my style.

Though it wasn't as easy, this didn't stop when I arrived in America. My family had moved to Beverly Hills in 1991—right when gangsta rap was taking over Los Angeles. I was already into that music and the West Coast rap look that came out of that movement. So I incorporated elements of that style into my look—Cortez Nikes and "wife-beaters" that I paired with lots of Persian gold jewelry, the bangles I'd had since I was a little girl, and a ring that I made for myself out of seashells.

I still didn't have a lot of money to spend on clothes, so I used my creativity to make the most of whatever I had. At the time, a lot of rappers were wearing necklaces that read "Africa," so my brother, Arta, and I made our own that said "Persian." Soon, everyone at Beverly Hills High wanted one of our Persian necklaces.

The rest of my style didn't go over quite as well. Unlike in Germany, where they appreciated my style more, in America people thought I was too different. Ironically, it started to feel like my style was preventing people from seeing the real me. They couldn't see past my clothes. This was the opposite of what I wanted to accomplish with my style! I wanted it to be a window to my soul, not a door.

In America, it took a lot of courage for me to be an individual. That wasn't easy as a fifteen-year-old, and I was tempted to scale back. In Europe, dressing wild and being myself was fun. Here, it was a drag. I didn't really care about fitting in, but I did feel a need to find my place in this new world.

At Beverly, the kids were divided into different categories: the Persians, the rich white kids, the jocks, and the black kids. Even within these categories, there were subcategories based on where you lived. The richest kids lived north of Sunset. The families with the least amount of money lived south of Olympic. There were gradations in between, but these were the two extremes.

Back in Germany, it was the refugee kids against the world, so I didn't understand this new social order. I didn't quite fit in anywhere. I looked like the Persian girls, but I definitely wasn't one of them. Eventually, it was my style that helped me find my people—the diverse group of artists and "vierdos" who became my friends. Being with them helped me get my feet back on the ground and gain the confidence to start building on my style again.

By then it was the late nineties, and as I started school at UCLA I was inspired by the street style I saw on the Venice Beach boardwalk. This added another dimension to my style. Now it wasn't just East meets West; it was East meets West with a little gangsta edge, a little hip-hop flash, and a little Venice Beach bohemian chic to top it off. When I traveled, I added elements to my style from around the world. Everywhere I went, I used what I saw to build more layers and new combinations for my style.

My outfits are now like beautiful patchwork quilts that represent every element of my life. Instead of wearing a Persian tablecloth as a skirt and a seventies skirt as a cape as I once did, now I'll wear a long, sequined, fuchsia kaftan with a fresh pair of Jordans and a turban. It's the grown-up version of what I've worn all along. And as I've begun to explore different sides of my personality through my style, I've found that I also have a need for simplicity at times. I'm a style extremist with two polarities. At once, I'm a maximalist in bejeweled heels, huge sunglasses, a bright kaftan, and a lot of gold and a minimalist in simple, sleek, structured clothing. Both looks represent me equally.

As I grow and evolve, so does my style. But no matter what I wear, when I get dressed in the morning I always feel the same giddy excitement knowing I have the freedom to be exactly who I am and no one else.

Being happy never goes out of style.

–LILLY PULITZER

STEP 1—DEVELOP YOUR PERSONAL STYLE

You may think that if you're not a fashionista or a movie star, your personal style doesn't matter. And of course I'm not saying it's important to wear expensive designer clothes, but expressing yourself through your style is important. It's not superficial. Developing your own style is a hugely meaningful way to feel good about yourself.

It all comes down to confidence, lover. When you feel like yourself in the clothes you wear, you feel more confident, period. I want the clothes you wear to make you feel amazing, to make you feel like *you*. I want you to use your style to share your spirit and energy with the world. This makes every day more fulfilling and fun.

Maybe you already have a fully developed sense of style, or maybe you've never even thought about it before. Either way is fine! You are going to use my rituals to develop a sense of style that will help define you in all of your unique and gorgeous golden glory.

Style is something very individual, very personal, and in their own unique way, I believe everyone is stylish.

–SALMAN KHAN

PRIESTESS POWER POINT: WORK WHAT YOUR MAMA GAVE YOU!

Learning to use what you've got physically and making it work for you is all part of developing your personal style. Some particular styles and cuts of clothing look better on certain body types than others. That's just a fact. Don't be afraid to play around with different styles to figure out what is the most flattering on your beautiful body.

I'm a curvy girl—always have been, always will be. Certain

things like A-line skirts and dresses look terrible on me. My body looks better in clothing that's more extreme—either with some structure, like tight-fitted clothing and wrap dresses, or thin, flowing items like my kaftans.

Instead of trying to hide the parts of your body you don't like, work on emphasizing the parts of your body that you love. If you have a beautiful, sexy neckline and a gorgeous back, wear a dress with an open back. If your legs are your thing, then wear a looser top and a shorter skirt. Everyone has something; no one has everything. Work your assets! There's no one else out there like you. Never be afraid to share with the world the things that make you special.

Develop Your Style Ritual

<u>You'll need</u>: a pin board or scrapbook, magazines, camera, folder
<u>Time allotted</u>: a few minutes each day

This is not quite a onetime ritual but more of an ongoing process. After all, it's not exactly possible to develop a full-fledged personal style overnight! The first thing you need to do is start to pay attention to the people and things you're attracted to. This might seem obvious, but a lot of people never take the time to develop a personal style or to even think about their style. They simply wear whatever's convenient or on sale. If this is you, that's okay, lover. But deep down, there is a part of you that longs to show itself to the world through your style. We are going to let her out!

When you watch a movie, what characters are you drawn to? What music do you like? Music and style are obviously closely connected. Musicians have given us some of the wildest, most amazing styles in the world, and you often feel a connection to certain music because you're drawn to the musician's style. No, you don't have to start dressing like Prince or Gwen Stefani! This is about becoming aware of what you like and are attracted to and then making it yours—not dressing up in a costume like it's Halloween.

What magazines do you like to look at? What stores do you drool over when you go window-shopping or walk around the mall? Which celebrities do you idolize or just enjoy watching? Which friends of yours have a sense of style that you admire? You may not even realize it, but you have your own unique tastes, lover. Start honoring them!

Over the next few days, every time you see some aesthetic that you're attracted to for any reason, take a picture of it. If it is a picture in a magazine, rip it out. Don't judge or second-guess yourself. You're drawn to these items for a reason. Honor that. Create a little style folder for yourself and put all those pictures in it. Include pictures of your favorite items in your own house or wardrobe! You probably have a couple of pieces that you wear all the time, the ones that define you. Take pictures of them and include them in your folder.

Once you have plenty of pictures in your folder—at least twenty or so—find a time to sit down and go through all of them. Find a comfortable place to spread out. Lay your pictures out on the floor or on a table or desk and take a look at them.

Are they all very similar or are they wildly different? Even if they're different, what do they have in common? Are there patterns you can detect between them? What do these images say to you—and about you?

How does looking at these images make you feel? Maybe you'll be surprised by some of them. They might be farther outside of the box or more traditional than you expected. That's okay! In fact, that's great, lover, because it means you're learning something new about yourself. Your inner voice is telling you something. Listen to it!

Use your pictures to create a bulletin board or scrapbook that's dedicated to your personal style. Keep adding things to it over time! And every time you go shopping or get dressed, ask yourself how you can incorporate elements from your scrapbook into your repertoire. How can you put those various pieces together? You can start as big or as small as you like, with individual pieces, a new haircut, or fully inspired outfits that show off your personal style.

Accessories are a good place to start exploring your personal style because it's easy to incorporate them into your existing outfits. Try wearing one of your classic outfits and adding a fun accessory—big earrings or one giant cocktail ring. This is a great way to start pushing the envelope with your style.

Remember, you do not have to have money to have style. When I started developing my personal style, I had no money. But I did have creative urges so strong I felt like they were explosive. They led me to create and discover new things. I made my own jewelry—the seashell ring I mentioned earlier and chokers that I made out of old Levi's 501s. I was doing it myself out of necessity, and now the idea of DIY is huge. Just this week, I saw a picture of Kim Kardashian wearing a denim choker that was a lot like one I made all those years ago!

The truth is that most people don't have money to buy designer clothes. The people who develop street style don't have money, but like me they have creativity. And then designers make expensive clothes for the masses based on their style. You can save a lot of money by just being original!

Unfortunately, lover, some people in your life might give you grief about your new style. Maybe they're envious or insecure about their own style, and seeing you flourish reminds them of their own failures. Do your best to ignore them. I know it's hard. But you have to be strong, with an undefeated spirit. Your own happiness and success are more important than what anyone else thinks.

When you embrace your freedom of expression and use it to let your inner voice speak out, other areas of your life will begin to open up, too. That's because you're finally being true to yourself. This is when the magic happens. You can't manifest all of the things you want and that are meant for you in this life if you're not being true to and honoring yourself. This goes for every aspect of your life—your mind, body, and spirit. The clothes you wear are a part of the physical element of your body. You are a work of art, not a mass-produced carbon copy. Don't leave your canvas empty! Use it to express something that's meaningful and beautiful to you.

My number one theory in life is that style is proportional to your lack of resources—the less you have, the more stylish you're likely to be.

—BETH DITTO

PRIESTESS POWER POINT: KEEP EVOLVING

Even after you develop your personal style, don't let yourself get stuck in a rut. Your personal style can (and should!) grow and evolve over time as you do. Never allow yourself to become complacent. If you've been rocking the same hairstyle and jeans that worked for you ten years ago, chances are that you aren't exploring and evolving in other areas of your life, either. Keep being curious and learning new things about yourself, and the universe will reward you with wonderful surprises.

STEP 2—STOP ASKING FOR PERMISSION TO BE YOU

My childhood wasn't easy, but in so many ways it was a gift because it taught me that there really is no such thing as normal. If 1970s miniskirts and tribal tattoos could be considered normal and then the next day, wearing a veil was the norm instead, then what was normal worth, anyway? Nothing, really. This made me fearless when it came to stepping out of the box with my style. I've learned that the box is an illusion. It's a set of rules that's artificially created. Babe, there is no box! Don't let anyone but you define who you are and what your identity is.

You know what's funny, lover? It's those people who are fearless and radically themselves who end up creating styles that other people follow. Look at some of the fashions that have become popular over the course of my lifetime: Michael Jackson's leather jacket, Prince's ruffled shirts and big hair, and Madonna's lace bustier draped with pearls. No one would have had the courage to wear those things if these icons hadn't done it first, and thank goodness they did! Where would fashion be today if these artists hadn't had the courage to express themselves?

I've seen this happen on a smaller level in my own life. A lot of the crazy stuff I used to wear ended up becoming popular just a few years later. When you have the confidence to rock something completely unique and outside the box, it gives other people the courage to do the same thing.

From watching *Shahs of Sunset*, some people think that all Persians wear a ton of stacked gold the way I do, but that wasn't always the case. On Season 1, people made fun of my style. They teased me for wearing all my gold, but now my entire cast is rocking huge gold rings and stacked bangles. At the very first group dinner, GG and I got into a ridiculous fight about the kaftan I was wearing. I was an easy target because I was different. But three years later, women around the world are rocking that kaftan.

To this day, when I wear something particularly expressive,

people tell me, "Only you can get away with that." Really? Why me? Or is the truth that I'm the only one who's willing to *try* to get away with it? I can't tell you how many messages I get from girls around the country who tell me that they love my kaftans but are afraid they can't pull it off.

This is crazy nonsense, lover! You do not need permission to be yourself! Stop waiting for some outside authority to tell you what's okay to wear and what's not okay. I'm not saying that you have to step out in some wild and crazy outfit if that's not you. This is about being you and finding your own unique style. If you are preppy or super-conservative, then rock your own version of that! It feels so good to face the world when your style matches the way you feel inside. Being yourself brings you peace of mind and so much confidence. That's what I want for you, lover.

> Style is whatever you want to do, if you can do it with confidence.
>
> —GEORGE CLINTON

Push the Boundaries of Your Self-Expression Ritual

<u>Time allotted</u>: however long it takes

<u>You'll need</u>: just the items in your closet

I bet that right now you have at least one accessory or item of clothing that you love but that you're a little bit afraid to wear. Maybe it's a shockingly short skirt, huge hoop earrings, or just a brightly printed top. Maybe it's nothing crazy at all but you feel like you'd be taking a risk if you wore it. I'd even bet that you kept these items after cleaning out your closet doing the home rituals.

Most people I know have at least a few items that are a little bit crazy for them. This is true even for me! My face jewelry is something that I only wear on certain special occasions. The rest of the time, it's too much of a distraction. But it does make me happy whenever I gather the courage to wear it. Continuing to push the boundaries is how I've become fearless. Pushing the envelope with your style will do the same for you.

Take some time to go through your closet, your drawers, and your jewelry box looking for items that match this description—the things you love but rarely (if ever) wear. Maybe you bust them out for New Year's Eve and that's it, or maybe they still have the tags on them from the store! Lay these items out and take a look at them. What do they have in common? How does looking at them make you feel?

Lover, you bought those things (and held on to them) for a reason. They spoke to you and told you something about yourself. Honor that piece of yourself by wearing them. How can you incorporate these items into the outfits you wear every day?

I'm not asking you to go from zero to a hundred all at once. Take small steps. Wear the big earrings with a conservative outfit for work, pair the miniskirt with a tamer top when you go out this weekend with your girlfriends, or try that sequined blazer with jeans and a tank. As you get more comfortable, keep taking baby steps toward outfits that are a fully realized expression of yourself, ones that make you feel amazing, as if your golden Inner Priestess is radiating out into the world through your style. Be fearless. Be you. That's when you know you're stylin' and profilin' for life!

Fashion is about dressing according to what's fashionable. Style is more about being yourself.

—OSCAR DE LA RENTA

Mini Style Ritual—Play Dress-Up

Earlier, you started playing dress-up before going out in order to boost your confidence and start feeling amazing in that gorgeous body of yours. This time, I want you to do it using only the wildest and most unique items in your wardrobe. That's right—put together every item that you set aside as being radically you into one outrageous outfit. Don't be scared! No one has to see this but you.

Now, put on the outfit and play your favorite music. Strut in front of the mirror and do a little dance. Be silly. Be outrageous! No one is watching; you have nothing to lose. You may be surprised by how good you feel and how amazing you look in the mirror. Remember that feeling the next time you're getting dressed to go out. You might be inspired to step up your style to the next level and show the world more of the unique and one and only you.

Fashions fade, style is eternal.

—YVES SAINT LAURENT

chapter nine

MANIFEST YOUR DREAM JOB

I've missed more than nine thousand shots in my career. I've lost almost
three hundred games. Twenty-six times, I've been trusted to take the
game-winning shot and missed. I've failed over and over and over again in
my life. And that is why I succeed.

—MICHAEL JORDAN

PRIESTESS PREVIEW

The rituals in this chapter will help you find your purpose and create a vision board so you can fully envision the life of your dreams. You can't get something if you can't imagine it, so this is a huge step toward manifesting everything you most want.

Let's be honest, lover—a lot of us have a complicated relationship with the idea of work. We all need to work to pay our bills, and today we spend more time at work (or working from home) than ever before. Yet so many of us are resistant to the very idea of work. We see it as a necessary evil or a means to an end. It's something we have to do, not something we want to do. We put in our time and look forward to the weekend, when we can finally have fun and spend time doing the things we're really passionate about. Think about the term "TGIF." This attitude is so pervasive in our society, but does it really make sense to spend the entire week waiting for it to end?

For many years I was torn between my true desire to pursue a career as an artist and the pressure I felt to make my parents proud with a professional career. In my culture, you get an advanced degree and then become a doctor or lawyer or something similar. It's as simple as that. It's just what you do, and I knew my parents expected me to do this, too. And sure, I probably could have. I was always a great student, and I graduated from UCLA with a double major in philosophy and psychology, thinking that I would use my education to become a therapist. But I just couldn't reconcile that path with my true passions. I loved talking to people and helping them to thrive. I'd always been good with people. But deep down I knew that

I wouldn't be staying true to myself if I became a therapist and gave up on my dreams of being an artist.

This was a major conflict for me. I already felt this intense pressure to make all of my parents' sacrifices worthwhile. How could I throw that away by failing to pursue a career that would make them proud? But on the other hand, would settling for a career that didn't light my soul on fire really be worth it? By example, my parents had taught me the value of true freedom. If it was worth leaving their families and entire lives behind in Iran in exchange for freedom, didn't I owe it to them to choose the freedom to chase after my wildest dreams? Of course becoming an artist was something I never could have even dreamed of doing in Iran, so maybe this was actually what my family's sacrifice was for.

I just knew that I would never be happy going to a job every day that I didn't love and that didn't fulfill me. What would be the point of that? Yes, of course I knew I had to make money. Nothing in life was ever handed to me. But I had learned first-hand that freedom was far more valuable than money.

But more important, my art was my life. I couldn't give it up. In many ways, I felt that my art had saved me. Throughout all the ups and downs of my childhood, I used my art as a way of making sense of the world around me. It was my therapy. This took many forms—photographs of the various things I observed, journals that I wrote in calligraphy in Farsi, German, and English, the clothing and jewelry that I designed and made myself, and of course my music. No matter what sort of art project I was working on, I channeled my hardships and my experiences into my creativity. This process was incredibly healing.

For many years, I kept my art and money separate in my mind. I was a puritan about my art and never wanted to alter it in order to make money. My art was *me*. I couldn't imagine changing that even the tiniest bit in order to make it more marketable or profitable. To me, that would have been selling out.

It was also nearly impossible for me to ask for money in exchange for my art. In my mind, my art was pure. It was something that existed in a different universe than money and paychecks and bills. At least, that's what I told myself. But the truth is that deep down I had internalized two false beliefs. The first one was the idea that I was bad with money simply because money wasn't something that my family discussed when I was growing up. I didn't have a bad relationship with money. I simply had *no* relationship with money. And as a result, I had no idea how to go about starting a career as an artist. The idea of fees and budgets and royalties was completely foreign to me.

The second negative belief I had internalized was that my art should be a hobby or a side project instead of a career. Throughout my life, countless people had told me that the idea of being an artist was ridiculous. I got this message loud and clear. Even my parents, who supported and loved me unconditionally, wanted me to take another path. My mom wanted me to get a PhD and thought I'd be throwing my life away if I pursued a career in art instead. I worried that if I didn't take her advice, I was disrespecting the sacrifices my parents had made for me.

It got to the point that when people asked me about myself or what I did for a living, I was afraid to say that I was an artist. The truth is, babe, deep down I also harbored a lot of insecurities about whether I was skilled enough to really make it as an artist. If the people who loved me were telling me to be a therapist, not an artist, maybe I wasn't as good as I thought I was and wanted to be. Once my mind started running in that direction, it was really hard to stop it. I knew how risky it was to try to make it as an artist. Most likely, I would fail. This idea was almost enough to stop me.

I found other ways to make money, but I never stopped doing my art. That's how much it meant to me. No matter what was going on in my life I was always engaged in different creative projects, even when I thought that no one would ever see them but me. One of the projects I was working on at that time was a music video with my best friend, Mr. Bunny. It was something we were doing just for fun and to express ourselves. Having an outlet for self-expression was (and still is!) vital. It keeps me sane.

We shot the video at our local grocery store and I taught myself how to edit it on my computer. It turned into a dope lo-fi Persian rap video that I thought was kind of fun and cool. The idea of making a Persian rap video seemed ridiculous and frivolous, even to me. But I couldn't stop myself. I was just so passionate about bringing my Persian culture into the world of pop culture and finding a way to combine the two. I felt that this was my purpose—the reason I was on this planet and why I had gone through everything I'd experienced in my life.

I also knew how lucky I was just to know what my purpose was. So many of my friends were still struggling to discover theirs or were stuck in office jobs with no time to wonder about their purpose in life. I had to gather all of my courage to go against what the people I loved and my deepest insecurities were telling me to do, but I couldn't walk away from my purpose. That wasn't an option for me.

I posted the Persian rap video on YouTube, expecting nothing. I honestly thought that only a few friends and family members would ever see it, but the video ended up going viral and leading to a ton of new opportunities for me to start earning a living through my art. I released seven singles on iTunes worldwide and performed my first live concert to a packed house at the El Rey Theatre in Los Angeles. As I moved forward making the most of these opportunities, I gradually gained confidence in my abilities, yet I still struggled to see myself as a good businesswoman or entrepreneur.

You may have noticed on Season 1 of *Shahs of Sunset* that I was terrible at asking for money to perform at a fashion show during New York's Fashion Week. By then, this had been going on for years. If I sold a painting, I felt so uncomfortable asking for a check. My art was *me*—it was my soul. It felt callous and gauche to ask for money in exchange for my soul. Money just wasn't something I knew how to talk about when it came to my art.

At the time, I didn't realize that this is actually supercommon among artists! This is why most writers, musicians, and artists have lawyers and agents. Most artists don't want to talk about money, so their representatives do it for them. As a young artist, I didn't know this. I didn't have a team of reps to support me, and I didn't know how to represent myself. I'd been successful at making money with other businesses, but art and business were always fragmented in my mind.

I knew that if I was going to make my art into a career, it would have to be a career that fulfilled me. And I wasn't going to be fulfilled if I didn't stay true to myself. This eventually became my definition of success—making money while pursuing my purpose and being true to my values and to myself. Gradually over time I saw more and more signs that I could find this version of success as an artist. I knew that success without fulfillment was nothing. My art fulfilled me. I may have been making money with it, but it was still a piece of my soul, and I couldn't ever let that become tarnished. I had to find my own way, and it ended up being so much more fulfilling (and more successful) than a shortcut ever would have.

It was when I developed Diamond Water that I finally struck that perfect balance between creativity and business. Although I had my own businesses before this and had made a good amount of money, Diamond Water was so special and different because it came straight from my rituals and my roots. This was unlike any business I'd been involved in before. And when I saw that investors wanted to give me money for something that was so close to my heart, I started to become more confident in myself as an entrepreneur.

I came up with the idea for Diamond Water—alkaline water infused with real diamonds—before alkaline water had really taken off. I knew from some friends in health circles that it was going to be big, and I found a way to connect it to my childhood and my culture to make it unique and personal. Like the Persian rap video, it blew up, but this time on a whole new level. Everyone loved the idea of Diamond Water, and I soon found people who wanted to invest in its development. It was still unreal to me that they wanted to invest in something that was such an integral piece of my roots and myself.

I went to those meetings with potential investors not knowing what to expect. And as I sat there listening to successful businessmen and -women offer me cold, hard cash to support something so personal to me, something inside of me clicked. Suddenly, I thought back to some of the projects I had taken on years before, back when I was in my twenties and still in school. I had gone to Thailand and found these really dope cotton fisherman pants. I became obsessed with them, and I knew that everyone in the States would love them, too. So when I got home, I figured out how to import the pants and I started selling them on eBay.

I kept that side hustle running for over a year while I was in school. It wasn't easy. I had to figure out how to import the pants, pay import taxes, set up an online store, and manage payments to different vendors. But to me, it was fun. No one gave me a guide or a road map. I just kept putting one foot in front of the other and figuring it out as I went, and it ended up being really successful.

I didn't stop there. When I did a semester abroad in India, I found beautiful silk fabric from Rajasthan that was used to make garments and bags. I brought home two huge trunks full of the fabric and sold it when I returned home. I didn't even do it for the money. It was fun for me. It was just me being me. But the whole time I still thought I wasn't good at using my creativity to make money. Lover, isn't it so funny and strange how we hold on to these false beliefs about ourselves, even when we come face-to-face with proof that they're not true?

Sitting in that meeting with the investors for Diamond Water, I realized that I had actually been an entrepreneur my whole life. I just didn't know it. I immediately started thinking differently about money and about myself, and my entrepreneurial spirit came bursting out of me. I had always had crazy, fun ideas, but they were always just a little bit outside of the box. I thought of myself as kind of weird and underground, but when I started to get positive reinforcement for my ideas, I realized that being out of the box is what makes me unique and special. That's my signature. I know how to take things that are deeply important to me and make them universal. That is a gift, and I had to learn to be grateful for it. Once I did, I gained so much more confidence to keep going.

So what was next? I always knew that I wanted to do something beautiful and empowering that celebrated the diversity of women around the world, and of course it was important for me to incorporate a piece of my ancient culture, particularly the specific part of Iran that my family is from. For many years, I'd been wearing kaftans that I had designed and had made just for me. People often commented about them and asked where they could buy one, but I brushed these comments aside. As my confidence grew, I became more and more inspired—and more devoted to pursuing the things that inspired me.

I decided to create a modern kaftan using a piece of my culture and making it accessible to a modern audience. To personalize it even more, I used prints from photographs I'd taken throughout my travels. Those photographs were a big part of how I processed the world around me. Soon, I found myself pouring every aspect of my life that I cared deeply about into my kaftans—my art, my culture, my style, and my inner confidence. I did all of this without thinking. It wasn't strategic. I was just following my intuition and my passion.

This project ended up being so personal to me that this time I didn't want to get investors involved like I had for Diamond Water. I didn't want to hand the reins of the business over to someone else. Instead, I decided to start small. If I succeeded, I wanted my family and me to be the ones who succeeded, not investors. So I spent two thousand dollars of my own money to have four styles of kaftans made. That was a big risk for me at the time, but I was in the zone and I felt it was worth it.

Jermaine and I happened to be going on a trip to Hawaii a few weeks later, so he took a few pictures of me in each of the kaftans after going for a swim. That was it. No fancy photo shoot or models—just me on the beach in a picture taken by my beloved. I wanted it to feel as real and authentic as it really was. When we got home from our trip, I posted those pictures on Instagram with a link to buy the kaftans and I wrote one sentence about what they meant to me. And just like that, Asa Kaftans was born.

Yes, people started buying the kaftans, and that was completely amazing. But it was even more important to me that people seemed to understand right away what I was doing. They could tell that it was from the heart. That meant so much to me, and it has translated into a level of success I never would have imagined. Sales for Asa Kaftans have taken off, but more important, women around the world constantly tell me how glamorous and beautiful they feel when they slip on one of my kaftans. That to me is true success. And the fact that my family is by my side helping me succeed and benefiting from that success right along with me is the icing on the cake.

It ended up taking me until I was in my thirties to find my true purpose and discover a way to combine everything I cared about into what is now a successful, fulfilling career for me and my whole family. It took a lot of work, a lot of courage, and a lot of passion to get here. But I was eventually rewarded for those efforts not just with money but also with fulfillment and joy. That's what I call a dream job.

Success is not final, failure is not fatal: it is the courage to continue that counts.

—WINSTON CHURCHILL

STEP 1—CHANGE YOUR ATTITUDE ABOUT WORK

Chances are, you don't have your dream job yet. That's okay! It may take a while to get there, lover. But if you have any sort of job right now that's paying your bills and putting food on your table, that is something to be grateful for. It bothers me so much when I hear people complaining about Mondays or praying for the week to fly by so Friday can hurry up and get here sooner. If you do this, you are wishing for your *life* to fly by. Your one life! Is that what you really want?

Yes, I know, your job may really be terrible. Maybe it's boring and mindless. Maybe your boss is mean and unfair. Or maybe your work is truly unpleasant or uncomfortable. If any of this is true, it's even more important for you to find things about your job to be grateful for. It may sound strange, but this all goes back to the energy you're putting out. When you're in a place of gratitude, the universe rewards you. It's fine if you're skeptical, lover, but what do you have to lose by trying it?

All of the energy you waste dreading Mondays and complaining about your boss is actually holding you back. It may seem counterintuitive, but practicing gratitude for the job you have today will change your energy and allow you to manifest the career of your dreams tomorrow.

Work is love made visible. And if you cannot work with love but only with distaste, it is better that you should leave your work and sit at the gate of the temple and take alms of those who work with joy.

—KAHLIL GIBRAN

Job Gratitude Ritual

<u>Time allotted</u>: 10 minutes—first thing in the morning!

<u>You'll need</u>: journal, pen

This ritual is really simple. When you wake up, stretch out your body a little bit. Sit up and grab a pen and paper or your journal. Close your eyes and think about the job you're going to today. Maybe you love it. Maybe you despise it. Maybe it's just okay. None of that matters.

Think of three things about your job that you are grateful for. No matter how much you may hate your job, you can think of three things if you really try. Maybe it's the simple fact that it pays your rent. That's no small thing! Maybe it's the vacation time you get. Or maybe it's the coworkers you enjoy going to happy hour with after work is over.

Write down the three things you're grateful for about your job, and then read them over out loud. Starting your day in this place of gratitude will dramatically shift your energy all day long—no matter what drama or stress you may face at work or at home. And this new energy will open the door for you to find your true purpose, which you'll do next. Feel free to repeat this ritual every morning or as often as you like, or just read your list over every morning to remind yourself of all the things you have to be grateful for.

This will also help you take pride in what you do. Whatever your job is, do it to the best of your ability, with a smile and a grateful attitude. This will raise your energy and put you in a place where you're more likely to get what you want out of life. Griping and going through the motions with a scowl and a bad attitude will get you nowhere, lover. Be that waiter who brightens someone's day or the babysitter who goes the extra mile to make a child laugh. You'll become a light in the world, and the universe will always repay you for shining brightly.

Your living is determined not so much by what life brings to you as by the attitude you bring to life; not so much by what happens to you as by the way your mind looks at what happens.

–KAHLIL GIBRAN

STEP 2—FIND YOUR PURPOSE

Everyone has been made for some particular work, and the desire for that work has been put in every heart.

–RUMI

Though it took a lot of courage for me to pursue art as a career, I was lucky to find my purpose at such a young age. I always knew that I was an artist—it just took some time for me to figure out how to turn that into a career. Some of us have a purpose that's obvious. We were born to do one thing, and it's apparent from the time we start walking and talking. Others of us are good at many things and take a bit longer to find out exactly what we were meant to do. Neither of these is better than the other. We each have our own path, our own unique story, and our own skills and passions. They are all equally valuable.

Unfortunately, our society doesn't always portray it this way. It's not hard to see how some skills are clearly valued more than others. But that doesn't mean they are really worth more in the ways that matter. That's because fulfillment is worth more than money. You can pursue a career that you're not passionate about just to make money, and you might enjoy it to some extent, but you won't feel truly fulfilled. Likewise, if you can earn a modest living doing what you really love, you'll feel like the richest person in the world.

Don't for one second believe that just because you're not Venus Williams or Beyoncé, you don't have a purpose that's just as meaningful as theirs. We each have our own purpose. Yours might not be as obvious. But everyone is amazing at something. You just have to find your thing. It's okay if you don't know what that is yet. This is a beautiful journey of self-discovery that may take some time. Let it take as long as it takes. There's no rush to get there.

After completing the Priestess Detox, you may find yourself coming closer to identifying your purpose. This is because you've begun peeling back the layers that you've built up over your golden Inner Priestess. Your golden self has all the information. She knows exactly what your purpose is. And the closer you get to her, the more you'll know what to do and how to do it. There's nothing you have to add or learn. It's all there for you already, buried beneath the surface like the gold coins in the foundation of my house. All you have to do is uncover that golden knowledge and find your way back home.

If you don't believe me, think of it this way. There's a purpose to everything in nature. Why would you be here for no reason? You are here for a very good reason, and deep down you already know what it is. But you've packed so many insecurities and false beliefs over that knowledge that you've lost touch with it. Trust that it's still within you. And it's your right to get back in touch with your purpose so you can feel powerful and strong and amazing in your life.

Remember, your purpose doesn't have to be glamorous. If we all had the same purpose, society would shut down. What you bring to the table is vital and needed. My mom is a nurse, and she's amazing at it. She's a caretaker. Her purpose throughout her entire adult life has been to take care of people and nurture them. She may not win any awards for doing her job, but my mom touches every life she comes in contact with. She's a healer. There's nothing more special or beautiful than that.

Maybe you have a desk job as someone's assistant and you're great at keeping him or her organized. Your purpose may be to become a master organizer and write bestselling books on this topic. Or maybe you're a stay-at-home mom who loves to bake for her kids. Well, how do you think Mrs. Fields got her start? Not everyone is a creative person, and that's not even the highest calling. Maybe you're creative or maybe you have a brilliant scientific mind. Maybe you're a natural caretaker or maybe you're superathletic.

What are you good at? What do people tell you you're good at? What lights your soul on fire and makes you feel amazing? You deserve to feel that way all the time. It's a natural defense mechanism for us to settle into a routine, tick-tock life. You check in, you check out, and you go through the motions like some sort of robot. No, lover! That is not the life for you. I want you to reach higher, to have a sparkle in your heart that fuels you to find your highest calling.

It's not an accident that musicians become musicians and engineers become engineers: it's what they're born to do. If you can tune into your purpose and really align with it, setting goals so that your vision is an expression of that purpose, then life flows much more easily.

—JACK CANFIELD

Find Your Purpose Ritual

<u>Time allotted</u>: 10 minutes, daily

<u>You'll need</u>: journal, pen

Okay, lover, it's time to start figuring out what really gives you joy. This is all about awareness. You're probably already naturally doing some things related to your purpose without even knowing it. The key is to start paying attention and observing yourself.

When do you feel excited and smitten with life? Is it when you master a new recipe, redecorate your bedroom, or throw a fantastic party? Or is it when you give a friend a great pep talk or spend the day with your sister's baby? Start paying attention to these moments. Every time you feel excited and giddy, stop and take note. Where are you? What are you doing? Who are you with? At the end of the day (or right in the moment if possible, so you don't forget) write down all of these moments when you felt excited and fully alive.

I bet that if you do this for a few days, you'll start to see patterns. You're using the same skills or doing similar things every time you get really excited. That's because you're doing something that's directly related to your purpose.

Once your purpose starts to reveal itself, begin to cherish that side of yourself. If you notice that you're happiest when you're baking, start baking pies for your friends and family. Maybe you can start selling them at a local market. Keep asking yourself how you can do what you love on a bigger and bigger level.

The world is a song, and you have to find your instrument so you can play along. We're all a part of this world, and we're all needed here. Don't just sit by the sidelines and watch. Join in! It would be such a waste to never find out what your purpose is. You are great at something, and you owe it to yourself and to this world to find out what it is. Remember, even thinking about your purpose is a luxury, a privilege. Previous generations didn't sit around thinking about their purpose in life. They were too busy trying to make ends meet! You have the chance to do this; don't take that for granted.

Even if now is not the time to pursue a new job or career, it's still important to find out what your purpose is. Simply being aware of it is empowering. We all go through different phases in life. Sometimes you're going full throttle and sometimes you're cruising. If you're cruising right now, that's okay. There's nothing wrong with that. But know that you have that throttle in you. Don't wait forever to use it. You don't want to wake up in ten years and realize that you missed out on contributing to the song. It's not as beautiful without you.

Let the beauty of what you love be what you do.

–RUMI

STEP 3—CREATE A VISION FOR YOUR LIFE

Now that you have an idea of what your purpose is, it's time to create a vision for your life. This is about taking responsibility for your one and only life. It's not enough to know your purpose. It's not enough to know what kind of job you want. Maybe you want to be a doctor. That's great. But what is being a doctor like? What does it feel like? What are the daily rewards and challenges? How does being a doctor fit into the rest of your life?

So many of us spend little time thinking about exactly what we want. We know what type of car or purse we'd buy if we had the money, but what do you want to get out of each day? How do you want to feel? If you don't take the time to answer these questions, the answers won't just magically appear. You'll go through your days, years will pass, and you'll wonder why you're not living the type of life you most want. The answer is simple, lover—you never took the time to really decide what you wanted out of life, so you never got it. Don't let that happen.

What is success? I think it is a mixture of having a flair for the thing that you are doing; knowing that it is not enough, that you have got to have hard work and a certain sense of purpose.

–MARGARET THATCHER

Life Vision Board Ritual

<u>Time allotted</u>: 1 hour

<u>You'll need</u>: your style pin board or scrapbook, magazines, glue or tape, pictures

If you can't see something clearly in your mind, you can't have it. You have to be able to see it and define it in order to make it a reality. Period. This goes for your soul mate, your ideal home, your personal style, and your dream job. It's why I had you write down the list of qualities you want in a soul mate and create a scrapbook or pin board that's a visual representation of your unique style. Now it's time to do the same thing when it comes to your career and the lifestyle that goes with it.

When we're unhappy with our jobs, we often start to believe that when we have the right career, everything else in our life will magically fall into place. But it doesn't work that way. Even the best job in the world will be exciting sometimes, challenging on certain days, and boring on others. And it won't fix the other problems in your life. You need to prepare yourself to inhabit every aspect of your dream job and lifestyle. And you can only do this by envisioning it fully.

Bring your materials to a quiet, comfortable place along with a cup of tea or something delicious and soothing. Get cozy and then close your eyes and start to imagine your life when you are living your purpose and have your dream job. Where are you living? Are you in the same house or somewhere else? A new city, perhaps? What does your home look like? How does it feel? Really take the time to picture it and imagine yourself there, living in this space.

When you're ready to move on, picture yourself getting ready for work. What do you wear? Are you heading to an office or working from home? How do you get to wherever you're going? Once you get there, what does it look like? What other people are there? What sort of vibe does this place have?

Now, ask yourself, what is the biggest challenge you'll face today at this job? Will it be a difficult client, a nasty coworker, or a tricky problem that you'll have to solve? How will you handle it? Then ask yourself, what will you do at this job today that will be particularly fulfilling?

How many hours will you work? What will you do when you're done? How will you feel after a day in this life? Will you be exhausted or energized? Why? When you feel that you've really experienced a day in this life, open your eyes. There's no rush here. Give yourself plenty of time.

Now try to find pictures that represent the way you felt during this visualization. Take some time to look through magazines or even your own photo albums for images that remind you of what you saw in your mind as you pictured yourself inhabiting this life. Add these pictures to your style pin board or scrapbook in any order you choose. Create something that brings back that sensation every time you look at it.

Defeat is not the worst of failures. Not to have tried is the true failure.

–GEORGE EDWARD WOODBERRY

STEP 4—NEVER GIVE UP

If you let your dreams die, you'll never be truly happy. I know you have bills to pay. Everybody does. And it's hard to pay your bills while pursuing your passion. I'm not telling you to just quit your job and hope for the best. Not at all. You have to be realistic and responsible. But it's just as important to never give up.

There is always a way to find time for the things you really care about. Maybe you have to work all day and then spend one hour at night pursuing your dreams. That's fine. Most successful people went through struggles in the beginning, and I'm sure you will, too. But they worked hard, they never gave up, and that's what ultimately made them successful.

Remember, starting something is always the hardest part, whether you're starting a new workout plan, a new business, or a new relationship. It takes courage. It takes risk. It almost seems insane if you really think about it! Most people can't get past it. In fact, it's not failure that holds people back—it's this fear of getting started. But if you just start anyway, the universe will reward you for putting it all on the line and going after what you want.

I know you're tired. I know you're overwhelmed. But I also know that you have that golden seed of inspiration and passion inside of you. Don't ever let that go. Put in the hard work and never let that muscle die. I won't lie—it's going to be hard, maybe even harder than you imagine. You need to really want it and be willing to do whatever it takes to make it happen. Talent is not enough. An amazing idea is not enough. Even your purpose is not enough. To really succeed, you'll need your purpose, hard work, and a little bit of magic. The first two are up to you.

Take up one idea. Make that one idea your life—think of it, dream of it, live on that idea. Let the brain, muscles, nerves, every part of your body, be full of that idea, and just leave every other idea alone. This is the way to success.

—SWAMI VIVEKANANDA

AFTERWORD

Why should I be unhappy? Every parcel of my being is in full bloom.

—RUMI

Lover, thank you so much for coming on this journey with me. I hope you're already starting to feel closer to your gorgeous Inner Priestess. Remember, unleashing your Inner Priestess will not happen overnight. It is a gradual, step-by-step process of getting to know yourself—a beautiful journey that I hope you will not rush through and instead take your time to fully enjoy. When it comes to any type of self-improvement—and anything in life, really—it's all about the process, not just the end result. Getting in touch with your golden self will feel magical, and if you approach every step with positivity and joy, the result will be that much more beautiful.

That positivity takes courage. It is scary to truly see things as they are and take responsibility for changing them. Some people who are bitter or afraid to change think that being positive means living in denial, ignoring the bad things, and claiming that everything is okay. Not at all. True positivity only comes from looking deeply into every dark corner of your life and shedding light on what you find. It takes bravery to face the truth. It takes strength to change. But I know you have both.

I am an extremely positive person, but do you think I got that way by blocking out all of the bad things that have happened in my life? Of course not. The only way for me to get through it was to face every challenge that came my way, and along the way I got stronger. I became a survivor. And I grew empowered when I saw firsthand how much control I actually had over my own life regardless of the circumstances.

Being positive simply means having hope—knowing that things can get better. This means that no matter how good or bad things may be right now, it's the perfect time to get excited about your life. During the darkest times of my life, I wouldn't have made it without hope. Having hope doesn't mean sitting back and wishing that your life will change. It means knowing that you have the power to change it. I hope that the rituals in this book will empower you with that positive outlook.

The happiest, most successful people in this world are the survivors, the ones who had no choice but to hold on to hope when it was all they had. This is what sets these people apart. Not talent alone. Not luck. It's talent plus persistence, discipline, and resilience. No matter what it looks like on Instagram, no one's life is perfect. Even the famous and super-rich have faced their own challenges and obstacles, just like you and me, but they never, ever gave up no matter how much the deck may have been stacked against them. The challenges you face don't matter; it's how you come out on the other end